C000049290

AMAZING AND EXTRAORDINARY FACTS

GREAT BRITAIN

GREAT BRITAIN

STEPHEN HALLIDAY

A Rydon Publishing Book
35 The Quadrant
Hassocks
West Sussex
BN6 8BP

www.rydonpublishing.co.uk
www.rydonpublishing.com

Revised edition first published by Rydon Publishing in 2019
First published by David & Charles in 2011

A CIP catalogue record for this book is available from the British Library.

ISBN: 978-1-910821-20-6

Printed in Poland by BZGraf SA

Images on the following pages adapted from work by:
p17 Mediatus; p25 Rainer Ebert; p27 Andrew Walker; p28 (bottom) Johnathon Ruchti; p72
Zoonabar; p28 (top) mym; p29 Tim Hallam; p32 (top) Colin Smith; p36 Roger W Haworth;
p37 Sebastian Ballard; p39 Saltmarsh; p47 Bubobuboo2; p48 David Ball; p53 Filipe Samora;
p58 Magnus Manske; p59 Ipankonin; p70 voltphoto; p83 Steve F; p88 meanone97; p95 Hilde
Vanstraelen biewoef; p96 Steve Popple; p105 Austen Redman; p113 Oxyman; p116 William M
Connolley; p119 Diliff; p141 Ewan M

CONTENTS

Kings, Queens and Princes 40

British Food and Drink 63

INTRODUCTION

No nation has had a greater impact on the world than that small island off the north-west coast of Europe on which an obscure Germanic tribe landed some time in the fifth century AD, shortly after the Romans had left. They joined the native Celts and were soon joined by other immigrants: Vikings from Norway and Denmark; Normans from France; Catholic Irish and, from France again, Protestant Huguenots, fleeing persecution in their native land. Then came Jews from Eastern Europe and Russia and, in the twentieth century, immigrants from every corner of the British Commonwealth, bringing with them ideas and skills as well as vocabulary which would help to turn the dialect of that Germanic tribe into the language of the world. Many aspects of British history and culture are taught to people in foreign lands. They are taught about Magna Carta, Parliamentary democracy and the rule of law but very few Britons know that the Common Law, one of Britain's gifts to the world, was the brainchild of a king who is better known for the murder of an archbishop. We take much for granted in our heritage. This book explores some aspects of that heritage that are less well known than they deserve to be.

Some of these are important, others are bizarre and some are both. For example Edward Jenner, who overcame the scourge of smallpox through vaccination would, in a more enlightened age such as ours, have been struck off the medical register for the way he went about his research. If Charles Darwin were an undergraduate at Cambridge in the twenty-first century he would probably be sent down for idleness and riotous behaviour. His father despaired of him. And is it really true that sauerkraut, pickled cabbage, not only helped Captain Cook to annex Australia to the British crown but also helped Britannia to rule the waves? And while we're on the subject of food, how was it that the British population was better fed in the Second World War than it has ever been, before or since?

When I came to look into some corners of our heritage I could scarcely believe some of the things I learned. Was the Méthode Champenoise really invented by a Gloucestershire country doctor whose main interest was in making glass bottles strong enough to contain sparkling wine? And was the kilt really invented by an English Quaker for the convenience of his Scottish charcoal burners? And why did Oliver Williams, Lord Protector, call himself Oliver Cromwell? And was Winston Churchill, with all his other responsibilities in World War II, really concerned with Britain's last witchcraft trial? And what was Adolf Hitler's brother doing in the "mountain city" of Liverpool before World War I? And how did The Beatles help to frustrate the attempts of General Gaulle to stem the onward march of English as the world's language? And where can you find a heroic firefighter buried close to Britain's favourite Poet Laureate? And why was it once fatal to impersonate a Chelsea Pensioner? And did George Stephenson, designer of the most famous of all steam engines The Rocket, really foresee that one day railways would run on electricity?

For the answers to these questions, and many more, read on.

Stephen Halliday

THE MAKING OF BRITAIN

An Island Nation?
Britain's continental connection

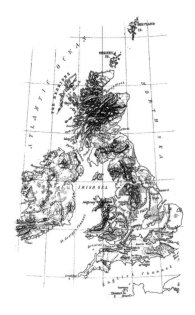

Until about 10,000 years ago Britain was joined to the continent of Europe via a land bridge, of which the most prominent relic is the Dogger Bank, *Dogge* being an old Dutch word for fishing boat. This lies under the North Sea between the east coast of England and the continent. Even now the water there is as little as 15 metres deep so when sea levels were 100 metres lower than at present Britain was not an island at all. In the previous 500 million years the land had been formed by violent geological activity. The mountains of the Lake District, for example, were formed by volcanic eruptions and its lake valleys were carved out by glaciers. As a result of all this activity and the fact that the land has alternately been submerged beneath seas and raised above them, the British Isles contains a greater diversity of geological phenomena than any region on earth of comparable size, with everything from volcanic rocks to marine deposits. The Lake District alone has three separate geological zones, made of completely different rocks, in less than 900 square miles. All we lack is really high mountains. Further north the Scottish landscape was altered in about 5,500 BC by a huge avalanche in Norway which precipitated a tsunami. This carried huge quantities of sand across the North Sea and deposited them at heights of up to twenty metres above sea level where they may still be found in an area extending from the Shetland Islands to the English border. And the process hasn't finished. The British Isles are tilting south-east towards Europe at the rate of 12 inches per century. And many features of our nation and its climate remain extraordinary.

FLOODING STOPS PLAY

A remnant of Britain's lost connection to the continent is the Goodwin Sands, a 10-mile-long sandbank six miles out to sea east of Deal. Its position, close to one of the world's busiest shipping lanes, ensures that it accounts for the world's greatest concentration of shipwrecks, one of them being the South Goodwin Lightship which was supposed to warn other ships of their proximity to this navigational hazard! The sands are also referred to as 'the widow maker' and 'the ship swallower'. In the 1970s there was a plan to build a third London airport on the sands but it was swiftly abandoned. At low tide the sands are clearly visible and for many years a tradition was observed of playing a cricket match on them. An attempt to re-enact this tradition for a BBC programme in 2006 had to be abandoned when the tide came in and the teams had to be rescued by the Ramsgate lifeboat.

In the centuries before the Roman settlements in the 1st century AD, Britain was almost entirely covered by forests. This explains why the prehistoric trackways follow high ground above the forested areas. The best example of this is the Ridgeway which runs from Overton Hill, near Avebury Stone Circle in Wiltshire to Ivinghoe Beacon, the highest point in the Chilterns, north of Aylesbury in Buckinghamshire. Its 87 mile length includes Wayland's Smithy, the White Horse of Uffington, and Segsbury Camp, all prehistoric in date but evidence that the trackway was well used by its mysterious travellers.

Southwest of the Ridgeway is the equally mysterious Stonehenge. Its origins are unknown though it was probably built in phases from 3,600 to 5,700 years ago using stones which came from as far as Pembrokeshire in Wales, 250 miles away. Early attempts to link Stonehenge with the Druids (of whom even less is known) have largely been abandoned. It has long been known that the stones are aligned with the midsummer sunrise and with the most southerly rising and northerly setting of the moon. More recent research has demonstrated more sophisticated alignments in accordance with the astronomical practices of ancient civilisations so it presumably served some kind of ritualistic function in

connection with astronomy. In 2010 tests on a skeleton found at the site, dating from about 1550 BC, suggested that it was that of a teenager from the Mediterranean region wearing a fine necklace of amber beads. This has led to speculation that it was a place of pilgrimage visited by wealthy individuals who could afford to make the journey, possibly for purposes of healing. Stonehenge was declared a UNESCO World Heritage Site in 1986.

Going to Extremes
A land of contrasts

The wettest place in Britain is Seathwaite, Cumbria, in the heart of Borrowdale in the Lake District. It receives about 140 inches of rain each year. The driest place is St Osyth, near Clacton in Essex, with about 20 inches a year. In some years it receives fewer than ten inches and is thus technically a desert.

The highest mountain in Great Britain is Ben Nevis, in Scotland, at 4,406 feet above sea level; in Wales it is Snowdon at 3,559 feet; in England Scafell Pike is the tallest at 3,162 feet.

The longest river in Britain is the Severn at 220 miles which rises in Wales but runs mostly through England. The longest river wholly in England is the Thames, at 215 miles. The longest river in Scotland is the Tay, at 120 miles; in Wales the river Towy is 64 miles long.

The lowest point in Great Britain is Holme Fen, south of Peterborough, 8 feet below sea level. No landscape point in Wales or Scotland is below sea level.

The windiest place in Britain is the summit of the Cairngorms in Scotland where, on 19 December 2008, a wind speed of 194 mph was recorded. This is too remote to be a suitable location for a wind farm but the world's largest wind farm was opened in the Irish Sea in September 2018. The Walney Extension has 87 turbines over an area of 56 square miles between Northern England and the Isle of Man. It can generate 659 megawatts which is enough to power almost 600,000 homes.

IS THE EARTH FLAT AT EARITH?

Much of the Fenland between Cambridge and the Wash lies below sea level and is kept dry by an elaborate system of drainage created in the 17th century. The most important element of this system is the Bedford Levels which run in two perfectly straight lines from Earith in Cambridgeshire to Denver, Norfolk, near the small town of Downham Market. They are named after the Duke of Bedford who promoted the scheme. In 1834 they attracted the attention of Samuel Rowbotham who used them to test his conviction that the Earth was flat. For nine months he lodged in a hut by one of the levels and aligned identical floats on it. If the earth was flat the floats, stretching over a distance of six miles, would exactly align. If the earth was curved then the more distant floats would fall away. The earth remained obstinately spherical, as it did when Lady Blount tried again in 1904.

Meet the Ancestors
Britain's first immigrants

Given the proximity of the Dogger land bridge to the east coast it is not surprising that the earliest evidence of human occupation of Great Britain has been found at Happisburgh, a hamlet on the north Norfolk coast. Flint tools dating from about 840,000 BC were found there in June 2010 following a similar find in Pakefield, Suffolk, five years earlier. The implements were probably made by pioneering nomads who crossed the bridge which linked Britain to the continent. They were not modern humans or even Neanderthals but a species known as *Homo antecessor*. The first Neanderthal remains, about 230,000 years old, were found at Pontnewydd in Wales in 1978. The first evidence of a modern human being, about 40,000 years old, was found in Kent's Cavern, near Torquay in 1927. A more sinister discovery was made in the Cheddar cave system in 2010 when the bones of what appears to have been a family group were found, with two adults, two teenagers and a baby.

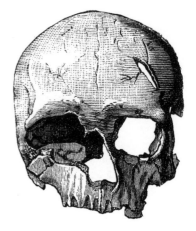

They appeared to date from about 12,000 BC and to have been expertly butchered, with knife marks on the bones suggesting they had been dismembered with a view to being eaten. So were our early ancestors cannibals? If so, were they driven to this by hunger, ritual or habit? The oldest domestic dwelling was found in August 2010, close to the east coast near Flixton, south of Scarborough. It dates from 8,500 BC, about the time that the land bridge between the east coast and the continent was inundated when the glaciers melted at the end of the last ice age. In the pages which follow we will examine some of the people and events which have influenced their descendants who still live in this extraordinary land.

United by Geography, Divided by History?
England, Scotland, Wales, Ireland

The British mainland retains two features which remind us that it was originally three separate kingdoms. Offa's Dyke was built by Offa, king of Mercia (reigned 757–96) to separate his kingdom from that of Powys, in Wales and it still marks the boundary between England and Wales for much of its 150-mile length. Wales, to which some of the Celtic population retreated during the Anglo-Saxon invasions from the 5th century onwards, retained its separate identity until its conquest by Edward I (reigned 1272–1307) who consolidated his conquest by building some of the world's finest medieval castles at Conway, Caernarvon, Harlech and elsewhere. An even more remarkable feature of the landscape is Hadrian's Wall, running from Wallsend near Newcastle to the Solway Firth north of Carlisle. Seventy-three miles long, it was built by the emperor Hadrian from 122 AD to mark the northern boundary of the Roman empire. It is the largest surviving Roman edifice in the world and at its western end it still roughly marks the boundary between England and Scotland. A path runs the length of the wall which, in 1987, was declared a World Heritage Site by UNESCO.

DO ALL ROADS LEAD TO ROME?

The most enduring Roman monument in Britain is the road system which we still use. The six A-roads that stretch out from London were all used by the Romans and built or improved by them. They link Roman cities and ports. The A1 (known to the Romans as Iter 8) runs from London to York (and now

5) runs from London to Carlisle and now goes on to Glasgow. Other roads linked important Roman settlements like Silchester, near Reading, Lincoln and Chester. Scotland's major cities were added later when the Ordnance Survey mapped mainland Britain. At the same time the Ordnance Survey numbered smaller roads in relation to the main A-roads. Thus smaller roads leading off the A1 begin with the digit 1 (A10, A12 etc.) and others follow this pattern. Cross country routes, like the A 272, are the exceptions.

on to Edinburgh), much of its length following the Roman Ermine Street. The A2, known to the Romans as Iter 3, links London and Dover, while the A3, which existed as a track before the Romans improved it (and built the Roman Stane Street nearby) connects London with Portsmouth. The A4 runs from London to the important Roman city of Bath and now goes on to Bristol and South Wales. The A5 (Watling Street) links London with Holyhead. The A6 (Roman Iter

Having turned his attention from Wales, Edward I failed to subdue his northern neighbour and the two kingdoms were united only when James VI of Scotland, son of Mary Queen of Scots, succeeded his cousin Queen Elizabeth to become James I of England. Many years earlier, Ireland had been annexed by King Henry II (reigned 1154–89). Henry, in effect, confiscated it from his subject Richard de Clare, 2nd Earl of Pembroke who had acquired lands in Ireland as a result of intervening in a dispute between two Irish chieftains.

This act of theft was supposedly validated by the *Donation of Ireland*, a Papal Bull (decree) by Adrian IV who was Pope from 1154–1159, the only Englishman to hold the post. There are doubts about whether there ever was such a Bull. Kings of England remained kings of Ireland, despite the protests of the Irish, until the creation of the Irish Republic in 1949 in which year George VI ceased to be king of Ireland.

THE BRITISH RED, WHITE AND BLUE

The Union Flag results from the combination of three national flags. The first is the flag of St George of England, a red cross on a white background, first adopted by the Crusader king Richard I (reigned 1189–99). Superimposed on that, in honour of King James I and VI, is the white diagonal cross (saltire) of St Andrew of Scotland on a blue background. St Andrew was traditionally crucified on a diagonal cross and was adopted as the patron saint of Scotland in 832 by the Scottish chieftain Oengus after he defeated a force of Anglo-Saxons near East Lothian. Oengus, while praying for victory, had seen clouds form in the shape of a saltire. Finally, following the Act of Union of 1800 which created 'The United Kingdom of Great Britain and Ireland', St Patrick's flag – a red saltire on a white background – was added to give the present Union Flag. St Patrick's flag dates from the 18th century and was probably an emblem of the Dukes of Leinster, Ireland's senior nobility. Wales was excluded from the party on the grounds that it was a principality, not a kingdom. The expression Union Jack, by which the flag is often known, dates from the practice in the Royal Navy of hanging the Union flag from the jackstaff, a vertical pole sited on a ship's bow.

The Tongue That Straddles the Globe
The pre-eminence of the English language

Who would have guessed that the language of an obscure Germanic tribe would develop into the most widely spoken language of the 21st century? It was brought to England by Anglo-Saxon settlers after the departure of the Roman legions from Britain in 410 AD. But it owes much of its success as an international language to its ability to absorb words and grammar from other languages. After the Norman conquest French became the language of government and court while Anglo-Saxon was the tongue of the common people. By the late 14th century, the time of Geoffrey Chaucer (c.1343–1400), a language recognisable as that which we speak today, predominantly Anglo-Saxon, had emerged as a language common to all classes. Chaucer's monarch, Henry IV, addressed Parliament in Chaucer's English rather than Norman French.

But there's more to English than Anglo-Saxon and French, with other languages represented, especially in place names. For instance, Dover is a survival of the ancient Celtic language which preceded the arrival of the Romans. It means 'waters', while Wendover in Buckinghamshire means 'white waters', a reference to the local chalk streams. The prefix Tr, sometimes followed by e, is also associated with Celtic origins, especially in Cornwall and Wales in names like Truro, Tredegar, Trelawney and Trevelyan.

Areas of Danish Viking settlement in eastern England and eastern Scotland contain many place names with Danish endings like –ston, –thorp, –toft, –thwaite, –holm and – ness. A glance at the maps of the areas concerned will reveal many more.

But English has been enriched by absorbing words from many other languages. The words 'bungalow', 'khaki' and 'jodhpur' were adopted from Hindi; 'barbecue', 'bonanza' and 'cockroach' from Spanish; 'ketchup', 'China' and 'silk' derive from Chinese words; 'anorak' is an Inuit word; 'candy' is taken from Arabic and its main ingredient 'sugar' is taken from the ancient Indian language Sanskrit.

'Bistro', surprisingly, is Russian; 'vampire' was originally Serbo-Croat; even the mysterious Basque language has given us the word 'bizarre'.

The rich tapestry of English

The decisive period for the formation of language was the age of the works of William Shakespeare (1564–1616) and the King James Bible (1611). Expressions from these works enriched English and, by their wide use, ensured that its influence spread. Here are a handful of phrases from the hundreds in daily use from the Bible:

Many are called but few are chosen (St Matthew)

A land flowing with milk and honey (Exodus)

The love of money is the root of all evil (Timothy)

Let us now praise famous men (Ecclesiasticus)

By their fruits ye shall know them (St Matthew)

Go and do thou likewise (St Luke)

The poor are always with you (St John)

Suffer fools gladly (Corinthians)

The salt of the earth (St Matthew)

The patience of Job (James)

Shakespeare made by far the largest contribution to the language of any single author. Here are some of his phrases:

Sweet are the uses of adversity (*As You Like It*)

Something is rotten in the state of Denmark (*Hamlet*)

Neither a borrower nor a lender be (*Hamlet*)

Cowards die many times before their deaths (*Julius Caesar*)

Go hang thyself (*Henry IV* Part I)

Love is blind (*The Merchant of
Venice*)
Thereby hangs a tale (*The Taming
of the Shrew*)
What's in a name? (*Romeo and
Juliet*)

SHAKESPEARE: GETS EVERYWHERE

*The late Anthony Burgess, author of
A Clockwork Orange, speculated
that Shakespeare himself contributed
to the King James Bible. Burgess
based this belief on clues in the text,
notably of Psalm 46. The Authorized
Version was being drafted in 1610, in
which year Shakespeare would have
been 46 years old. In the King James
version of Psalm 46 the 46th word
in the text is shake. The 46th word
from the end is spear. Distinguished
contemporary writers were used to
polish the text and none was more
famous than Shakespeare at that
time. It's an intriguing thought.*

Other common expressions
have less illustrious origins, some
quite sinister. 'Money for old rope'
derives from hangmen's practice of
supplementing their incomes by
selling ropes used for executions;
'men of straw' has an equally sinister
origin. In the 14th century men
would stand outside law courts with
pieces of straw protruding from their
pockets or shoes to indicate that they
were prepared to give evidence for
whichever party would pay them.

'Bobby', 'Old Bill' and 'copper'
in reference to the police can all be
traced back to the early days of the
police service. The Metropolitan
Police was set up by the Home
Secretary Sir Robert Peel by an Act
of 1829 and the expression 'Bobby'
is a reference to 'Bobby Peel'. In
Ireland the police are still sometimes
referred to as 'Peelers'. The following
year King George IV died and was
succeeded by his brother William
IV. The new police constables were
issued with a wooden truncheon,
each encircled by a thin band of
copper on which was engraved W
IV R to signify that they were acting
under the authority of King William.
By extension the copper band came
to be associated with the constables
themselves, hence 'copper'. Finally,
King William IV was often referred
to as 'Silly Billy' or 'Old Bill' and this

term also came to be attached to the police who acted in his name.

The Sheriff's Posse – which we associate with cowboys and the American 'wild west' – originated in Anglo-Saxon England when all males aged twelve or over were organized into groups of ten families, or *tithings*, whose members were responsible for identifying and apprehending any other member of the tithing who had committed a crime: a kind of Anglo-Saxon neighbourhood watch. After the Norman conquest this was supplemented by the practice of hue and cry whereby the Sheriff of the County, who was responsible to the king, could invoke his *Posse Comitatus* (literally 'power of the county') to require fellow citizens to pursue and arrest a criminal.

The New *Lingua Franca*

Until the 19th century French was accepted as the international language of diplomacy but in the following century English gradually replaced it. The expansion of the British Empire, to a point where it comprised about one quarter of the world's population, was followed by the expansion of

American multinational companies after World War II, carrying with them the language which had become the tongue of America before the War of Independence (to this day the United State does not have an official language). In the 1950s French president General de Gaulle and the German Chancellor Konrad Adenauer, neither of whom was pre-disposed to the British or Americans, each agreed to promote the language of the other in their schools. It didn't work. The young people of France and Germany preferred the music of The Beatles and the Rolling Stones to their home-grown versions and chose to learn English, the language of popular culture and international business.

Hundreds of Years of Hurt
Britain's beautiful game: football

Football or games like it have been played from time immemorial but was long regarded as a source of disorder. In 1314 Edward II issued an edict to Londoners to the effect that 'Forasmuch as there is a great noise in the city caused by hustling over large balls, from which many evils may arise, we forbid, on behalf of the king, on pain of imprisonment, such game to be used in the city in future.' Royal displeasure continued to be expressed over the following centuries and the game became respectable only when it began to be played in the public schools which expanded rapidly in the 19th century. Since there was little contact between schools, owing to difficulties of travel, each school developed its own rules. For example, some permitted handling the ball and some permitted hacking opponents' shins. These differences became a problem when the pupils of different schools found themselves playing with one another at universities and games often ended in violent brawls, as in medieval times.

The problem came to a head at Cambridge in 1848 when two boys from Shrewsbury school, Henry de Winton and John Charles Thring, called a meeting of representatives of many schools at Parker's Piece, an open space in Cambridge, to agree a common set of rules. This made the game very popular at Cambridge in matches between the colleges and

in 1862 Thring drew up a set of ten rules for wider use. Some of them seem curious now, for example:

Rule 2. Hands may be used only to stop a ball and place it on the grounds before the feet

Rule 3. Kicks must be aimed only at the ball [i.e. not at opponents!]

Rule 5. No tripping up or heel-kicking allowed

Rule 9 states that 'A player is out of play immediately if he is in front of the ball' which means that one is very restricted in passing the ball forward, more like Rugby than modern football. An alternative code was agreed for those who wished to handle the ball more freely, based on the practice at Rugby school. The rules of association football were later developed both at Cambridge and, in 1863, at a meeting at the Freemason's Tavern in Great Queen Street, London, which is sometimes cited as the origin of the game which is now, by some distance, the world's most popular. But it all started on Parker's Piece, in 1862, where football is still played.

EXTRAORDINARY PLACES

Many places in Britain can claim distinctions of one kind or another. Each of the communities or locations listed below has at least two claims to distinction of an unusual kind.

A Hitler Among the Scousers
Liverpool attracts all sorts

L iverpool has Britain's largest cathedral which is second in size only to St Peter's, Rome, in the Christian world. The city also has the largest clock faces in Britain on the Royal Liver Building, one of the three graces on the waterfront, the others being the Port of Liverpool Building and the Cunard Building, elegant examples of early 20th century architecture when Liverpool was at the height of its prosperity and second only to London as the world's greatest port.

LIVERPOOL PRONOUNCED 'MOUNTAIN CITY': ITALIAN OPERA – SCOUSE STYLE

The Italian composer Gaetano Donizetti (1797–1848) was a great admirer of Britain but he sometimes allowed his imagination to get the better of his judgement. He wrote 75 operas, some of them very fine such as **Anna Bolena, Maria Stuarda** *and* **Lucia di Lammermoor,** *all based on figures in British history or* *literature. But one of the most curious is* **Emilia di Liverpool,** *about a young woman of that name who elopes with her lover to the beautiful mountain city of Liverpool in whose vertiginous terrain she finds refuge from her shame. It is rarely performed but in 2008 it opened the festivities which marked Liverpool's celebration as European Capital of Culture, receiving an enthusiastic reception from its audience of Scousers who had never noticed that they lived on a mountain, believing the port of Liverpool to be at sea level.*

In the first decade of the 20th century Liverpool was for a short time the home of Alois Hitler, half-brother of the rather better-known Adolf. Alois married an Irish woman called Bridget Dowling and they lived at 102, Upper Stanhope Street, Toxteth, with their only child, William Patrick Hitler, until Alois abandoned the family and returned to Germany in 1914 where he remarried bigamously. Bridget and William Patrick emigrated to the United States in 1939 and Bridget tried to cash in on the notoriety of her brother-in-law by claiming, in a manuscript called *My brother in law Adolf*, that Adolf Hitler had visited the family in Liverpool in 1912 to avoid conscription into the Austrian army. There is no reason to believe that this is true and the book was never published. Ironically the family home in Toxteth was destroyed in the last German air raid on Liverpool in January 1942.

Want to Relocate Your Old Capital City?
Just call Boadicea

Colchester in Essex is Britain's oldest city: the first Roman town in Britain and its first capital (called Camulodunum) until it was sacked in AD 60 by 30-year-old Queen Boudicca (Boadicea), after which the capital was moved to Londinium. Colchester Castle, built by the Normans shortly after their invasion and conquest, also has the largest keep in Europe, one and a half times larger than the Tower of London's White Tower.

My Horse for Your Daughter?
Fair trading at Appleby's horse fair

With a population of fewer than 3,000, Appleby in the county of Westmorland was the smallest county town in Britain until Westmorland was merged with Cumbria in 1974. It also holds the biggest horse fair in the world every June. It was established in 1685 and is a traditional gathering place for gypsy families to trade in horses and, in the case of eligible younger people, to seek partners.

Colchester Castle

The Second City of the Empire
Glasgow's green spaces and curry houses

In the 19th century Glasgow was the second largest city in the British Empire, exceeded in population only by London. It had more parks than any city of comparable size (today it has over 90) and it is now the curry capital of Britain, with 50 per cent of Glaswegians eating curry at least once a week.

St Andrews Greensted-juxta-Ongar

Ancient Essex Man a Devout Breed
The oldest churches in Britain

Canterbury has the oldest school in Britain in King's School, reputedly founded by St Augustine in 600; England's greatest medieval shrine, that of Thomas à Becket, murdered in 1170; and England's oldest church still in regular use, the church of St Martin, the date of whose foundation is uncertain but probably dates from the late 600s. Probably older and still occasionally used is the remote little church of St Peter on the Wall, Bradwell, in Essex, built by St Cedd in 654. The oldest timber church in the world is also in Essex, St Andrew's at Greensted-juxta-Ongar, which has been dated using dendrochronology to 845.

Christ Church College

Fractious French Exchange Programme Prompts Foundation of Britain's Oldest University
Oxford's dreaming spires

Oxford has Britain's oldest university. Its precise origins are unclear. Some date it from 1167 when Henry II's dispute with French king Philip Augustus made it impossible for English students to study in France; others suggest 1186 by which date Geraldus Cambrensis (Gerald of Wales) is recorded as lecturing to students. Oxford also has Britain's smallest cathedral which doubles as the chapel of Christ Church, Oxford's largest college. Cardinal Wolsey planned to found Cardinal College as a monument to himself and, in preparation for this, took over the church of St Frideswide. When Wolsey fell from favour with Henry VIII the king assumed responsibility for the foundation, named it Christ Church and gave St Frideswide to the first bishop of the new diocese of Oxford to be used as his cathedral while it continued to serve as chapel to the new college.

The Scottish Missionary Position
Cross-roads of early British Christianity

Iona, a small island off the Isle of Mull on the western coast of Scotland, is home to the oldest Christian site in Britain. It became the home of St Columba when he was exiled from Ireland in 563. Columba brought Christianity to Scotland and to the English kingdom of Northumbria thirty-four years before St Augustine arrived at Canterbury from Rome in 597. It is likely that the beautifully illuminated *Book of Kells,* an 8th century text of the gospels, was produced at Iona and taken to Ireland to escape Viking raids. It is now in the library of Trinity College Dublin. Columba founded a monastery that later became the site of Iona Abbey which was rebuilt by the Iona Community from 1938. Led by George MacLeod (1895–1991) it re-established the traditions of Celtic Christianity and remains a thriving Christian community.

Linenopolis to Metropolis
Belfast's Titanic shipbuilding feats

B elfast was so dominant in the Irish linen industry that at the beginning of the 20th century it was briefly the largest city in Ireland. It has a proud engineering heritage and is still home to Harland and Wolff, once the biggest shipyard in the world, which in 1912 launched the ill-fated *Titanic*. It was also the builder of other famous British ships such as the cruiser HMS *Belfast*, now moored on the Thames opposite the Tower of London, and P&O's *Canberra* liner. It was the home of Dr William Drennan (1754–1820) who in 1795 first used the term 'the Emerald Isle'

to describe Ireland. In 1855 it was the home of Anthony Trollope when he completed his first Barsetshire novel *The Warden* while he was working for the Post Office. Belfast is the administrative and financial capital of the province of Northern Ireland and is the centre of highest population with about 280,000 citizens.

'The Very Ramparts of Heaven'
Ancient Lincoln in need of repair

L incoln Cathedral has the highest cathedral tower in Europe at 271 feet. Until 1549 it was the tallest building in the world, higher than the Great Pyramid but in 1549 its spire, 525 feet tall, collapsed. In the form of the 3rd century Roman Newport

Arch Lincoln also has the oldest arch in Britain still used by traffic. It also has the Jew's House dating from the mid-12th century which is reputed to be the oldest surviving domestic building in Britain, now a restaurant.

Wales's Hidden Treasure-Trove
Local boys done good, too

Porthmadog, Gwynedd, is the terminus of the world's oldest independent railway company. The Ffestiniog Railway was created by Act of Parliament in 1832 to convey slates from the quarries and mines at Blaenau Ffestiniog to the port of Porthmadog. It remained independent when the rest of the railway network was nationalized in 1948 and survives as a visitor attraction. During World War II the slate mines, which maintain a constant temperature and humidity, were used to store art treasures from the Tate Gallery and the National Gallery in London. Nearby Tremadog contains Lawrence House, the birthplace of T E Lawrence (Lawrence of Arabia), and Criccieth, the home of David Lloyd George, prime minister and a famous son of Wales.

Water Way To Have A Good Time
Boating at altitude

Llangollen, Denbighshire, is home to two remarkable memorials to British engineering excellence. The Llangollen Railway opened in 1865, was closed in 1962 and reopened in 1986 as a result of the determined efforts of volunteers. It is now one of the most popular steam railways in Britain, carrying passengers along the valley of the River Dee. Nearby is the extraordinary Pontcysyllte aqueduct, which carries the Llangollen Canal across the Dee valley. Completed in 1805, it is the longest and highest aqueduct in Britain, a Grade I listed structure and a World Heritage site. Built by Thomas Telford and William Jessop it consists of a cast iron trough over 1,000 feet in length, 126 feet above the river valley below. Nervous passengers on narrow-boats are advised to remain below deck when crossing the aqueduct since there is a towpath on only one side and a sheer drop on the other.

Pulling Out the Stops
Alfred the Great's old organ

Malmesbury in Wiltshire is England's oldest borough, its charter having been granted by Anglo-Saxon king Alfred the Great in 880. It also had the very first church organ in England, installed in Malmesbury Abbey in 700,

driven by bellows. Moreover the Old Bell hotel, close to the abbey, was built around the remains of a Saxon castle in 1220 as a guest house for the abbey and, having been in use ever since as a lodging house or hotel, can claim to be Britain's oldest hotel.

Dodgy Handshakes and Umpteen Takes
Rosslyn hits the limelight

Rosslyn Chapel, in the small Scottish village of Roslin, south of Edinburgh, was built in the middle of the 15th century and contains some of the finest medieval carving in the world. It has also gained unsought fame, and many visitors, through its association with the Knights Templar, Freemasonry and the Holy Grail as a result of Dan Brown's bestselling novel and film *The Da Vinci Code*.

Shells of the Non-Collectible Variety
Scarborough takes a pounding from the sea

Scarborough in Yorkshire became the first British seaside resort as a result of the discovery of spa waters there in the early 17th century. It was the first resort to use bathing machines, in 1735. But in 1914 Scarborough entered the record books for less desirable reasons when it became the first British town to be shelled by the German fleet during December 1914 in World War I. With its seaside neighbours Hartlepool and Whitby also struck by German battlecruisers, 137 people were killed and nearly 600 wounded.

Sixty Warriors to the Square Inch
Scones for afters?

Perth was the site of one of the most extraordinary episodes in Scottish history, the Battle of the Clans. In September 1396 a staged battle was fought, in the presence of spectators including King Robert III of Scotland, between the Chattan Confederation (the Mackintoshes, Macphersons and other clans) and their traditional enemies whose identity is far from clear but may have been their traditional rivals the Clan Cameron. It is not even clear what the dispute was about. Thirty warriors from each side fought on Perth's North Inch, now a peaceful and charming park within the city. The Chattans were declared the victors when they killed all but one of their opponents for the loss of nineteen of their own warriors. Nearby is Scone Abbey, home of the Stone of Scone on which Scottish kings were traditionally crowned. Long a ruin the abbey was further damaged in September 2010 when a white van collided with a 500-year-old archway which was the best-preserved relic of the medieval building.

Morning Campers!
The bracing charms of Skeggy

S kegness, situated on the east coast of England in Lincolnshire, saw the opening of the first Butlin's holiday camp at Easter in 1936. The first visitor was Freda Monk who found the new facility deserted when she arrived until she found the camp manager who explained that it wasn't opening until the following day. For Britons who had been used to seaside holidays in boarding houses where they were thrown out after breakfast, regardless of the weather, the Butlin's holiday camp – with four meals a day, chalet accommodation, knobbly-knee competitions and jolly Redcoats – was a revelation. The weekly charge was £3 a person – roughly an average week's wages. By 1938 Britain had 150 holiday camps, helped by the passage that year of the Holidays with Pay Act. In March 2005, Skegness was declared the best retirement place in Great Britain following a survey by *Yours Magazine*. Sixty likely towns

were surveyed against such criteria as house prices, hospital waiting lists, crime rates, council tax rates, activities and attractions, weather patterns and ease of transport. *Lonely Planet's* Great Britain guide wrote that it had 'everything you could want' in a seaside resort. Nevertheless in July 2008 Boris Johnson, newly elected as Mayor of London, upset some people in an article in the *Daily Telegraph* in which he declared, 'Stuff Skegness, my trunks and I are off to the sun.'

HI-DE-HI!, SPARTAN SOCIALIST STYLE

The first English holiday camp predates Butlin's by 30 years. It was established in Caister, near Great Yarmouth in Norfolk, by John Fletcher Dodd, a grocer and founder member of the Independent Labour Party. In 1906 he bought a house near the seafront and invited some fellow socialists from the East End of London to occupy some tents in his garden. The enterprise expanded, with wooden chalets and a dining hall which could accommodate 500 people. It was run on strict lines with bans on alcohol, smoking, gambling, improper language and noise after 11 pm. Anyone infringing the rules was asked to leave. Visitors included leading socialists like Herbert Morrison, George Bernard Shaw and Keir Hardie. In 1924 the cost of staying at Caister was a guinea (21 shillings, or £1.05 in modern decimalized sterling) for a week. The camp expanded during the 1930s though the atmosphere must have been very different from that at Butlin's up the coast! By the 1950s the camp was attracting a thousand visitors a week. The Dodd family eventually sold it to Haven holidays and it continues to thrive, though with a less severe regime than that of its founder.

Cambria Ne'er Can Yield!
Sieges of Harlech

Harlech in Wales's Cardigan Bay is home to one of the fourteen castles built by King Edward I in his conquest of Wales. Its design, consisting of two rings of concentric walls, makes it almost impregnable and it was situated so that it could be supplied from the sea and thereby withstand sieges. Nevertheless in 1404 Owain Glyndwr managed to take the castle after a long siege and for the following four years it was his headquarters and the de facto capital of Wales. From 1461–1468 it held out against the longest known siege in British history, remaining the last Lancastrian stronghold in Wales during the Wars of the Roses, a feat which inspired the song *Men of Harlech*. Nearby are the Roman Steps, a staircase cut into the mountain. Traditionally associated with the Romans, who quarried slate in the area, their precise origin is a mystery.

One-Way Ticket to the Eternal Underground
Woking: gateway to the Gods

In 1850, alarmed by the overflowing burial grounds of London churches, Parliament purchased 2,000 acres of land at Brookwood, near Woking in Surrey. The London and South-Western Railway constructed adjacent to Waterloo a special station for mourners and two stations at Woking Necropolis station (now called Brookwood), one for use by Anglicans and one for Nonconformists. The new cemetery was consecrated by the Bishop of Winchester in 1854 and since that time almost a quarter

of a million people have been buried there. It is the largest cemetery in Europe and contains separate sections for groups including Latvians, Chelsea Pensioners and Muslims. Dodi Fayed was initially buried there but was later moved to a grave in the grounds of the Fayed family home at Oxted in Surrey. Woking is also the home of the first purpose-built mosque ever built in Britain, the Shah Jahan Mosque, which opened in 1889.

Oldest and Oldest
Berrow's Worcester Journal

Worcester is noted for its beautiful cathedral, its porcelain and its association with Edward Elgar. However it is also the home of the world's oldest daily newspaper. Founded in 1690 as the *Worcester Postman* it became *Berrow's Worcester Journal* when the new proprietor, Harvey Berrow, changed the name in 1753. The cathedral also

contains the oldest effigy of an English monarch, that of King John, who was buried there in 1216.

The Venice of the West (Midlands)
The birthplace of British industry

Birmingham – England's second-largest city – has a greater mileage of canals than any other European city, since it is the hub of the British canal system. It was also the home of the first large-scale manufacturing establishment in the world: the Soho works of Matthew Boulton and James Watt whose mechanized plant was a blueprint for similar establishments which underpinned the Industrial Revolution pioneered in Britain.

LEGGING IT

The British canal system has added two expressions to the language. Navvies, or navigators, were the armies of labouring men, often Irish, who dug out and constructed the canals in the 18th and 19th centuries and went on to build the railways. 'Legging it' referred to the process by which canal boats were manoeuvred through tunnels, where horses could not tow them. Men known as 'leggers' would lie on planks set across the boat and 'walk' or 'leg' the boat along by pushing against the walls (or roof) of the tunnel with their feet. Britain still has 2,000 miles of inland waterways – about 80 per cent of the extent during the heyday of the system – and about 27,000 boats though nearly all are now used as dwellings or pleasure craft rather than for conveying freight which was their original purpose. One of the canal system's most peculiar features is Weedon Bec, on the Grand Union Canal near Daventry in Northamptonshire. Constructed during the Napoleonic Wars as a small-arms ordnance depot, it was designed to double as a refuge for the royal family who would evacuate there from London in the event of invasion. It is far inland from the coast but accessible because of the canal which serves it. The complex is now used as stores and workshops for the many small firms in the area.

Tearing Down the Walls
Derry's identity crisis – all in the name of religion

What's in a name? Quite a lot if the name is Londonderry. One of the oldest inhabited towns in Ireland, it was originally called Derry, the old Irish word for the oaks which grew in the area. In 1613 James I, who wished to encourage English and Scottish Protestants to settle there, changed the name to Londonderry. The name has been a matter of dispute between the Catholic and Protestant citizens of Northern Ireland ever since. The district of Derry and Strabane was created in 2015, subsuming a district created in 1973 with the name "Londonderry", which changed to "Derry" in 1984. It

was the last walled city to be built in Europe, the walls being constructed between 1613 and 1619 to reassure the English and Scottish settlers who were fearful of their Catholic neighbours. In 1867 it became the home of Mrs C F Alexander (1818–1895), creator of well-known hymns such as *Once in Royal David's City* and *All Things Bright and Beautiful*. Her husband was the Bishop of Derry.

The Heart of the British Film Industry
Ealing in black-and-white

Ealing, in west London, was the subject of the first English census in 1599. This was a list of all 85 households in the village giving the names of the inhabitants, together with their ages, relationships and occupations. No-one knows why it was taken, 202 years before the first full British census in 1801. The results may be seen in The National Archives not far away in Kew. Ealing is also the home of the world's oldest film studios. Established in 1896, it later became associated with the Ealing comedies such as *Passport to Pimlico* and *The Lavender Hill Mob* as well as with classic war films like *The Cruel Sea*. From 1955 to 1995 the studios were owned by the BBC which made such 1970s series as *Colditz* and *Porridge* there. In 2000 the studios were bought by a new owner and have been used for making such films as the 2002 production of Oscar Wilde's *The Importance of being Earnest*.

The Underground Church
Resting place for a poet and a heroine

Trebetherick in Cornwall contains the church of St Enodoc which for almost three centuries was submerged in drifting sand except for a portion of the tower. Once a year the rector of the nearby parish of St Miniver would descend through an opening in the tower beneath the bent steeple, accompanied

by parishioners, to conduct a service in order to keep the church in use and, importantly, maintain its right to collect tithes. By 1864 the dunes were cleared away and the church has remained open ever since. The small churchyard contains two remarkable graves. The first is that of the former poet laureate Sir John Betjeman (1906–1984) who loved Trebetherick. The second is that of Fleur Lombard (1974–1996) the first female fire-fighter to die on peacetime active service while tackling a fire which arose from an arson attack in Bristol. She was posthumously awarded the Queen's Gallantry Medal.

KINGS, QUEENS AND PRINCES

These islands have had more than their share of colourful rulers. Kings, queens and princes have followed one another over the centuries in a rich tapestry of inheritance, invasion, war and murder – within which truth has often been interwoven with myth. Regal or roguish, here are some of the more celebrated and notorious royals.

Murderer Assassinated by Shakespeare
The Princes in the Tower

Since William the Conqueror there have been 41 monarchs of Great Britain, including the present Queen Elizabeth II. They include one dual monarchy (William and Mary, who reigned from 1689 until William's death in 1702), and two kings who were never crowned: Edward V, one of the murdered 'Princes in the Tower'; and Edward VIII who abdicated in December 1936 after reigning for less than a year. However, some of

the coronations which did take place were, to say the least, eventful.

The Princes in the Tower were almost certainly murdered, probably on the orders of their uncle Richard III. Other candidates have been largely eliminated because Richard III had the unparalleled misfortune of having his character assassinated by William Shakespeare in one of his most memorable plays, *Richard III*. However the princes did not disappear completely. During the reign of Henry VII, who defeated Richard III at the battle of Bosworth in 1485, young men occasionally appeared claiming to be one of the princes or a close relative and thus, by some people's reckoning, the rightful king of England. In 1491 one of these appeared in Cork and announced that he was Richard, Duke of York, the younger brother of Edward V. He was recognized by some European monarchs who were enemies of Henry VII and landed in Cornwall in 1497. His rebellion swiftly petered out and Henry spared his life when the impostor confessed that he was really Perkin Warbeck, born in Tournai, France. He was sent to the

Tower but escaped. Henry, by now thoroughly fed up with him, had him hanged at Tyburn. A more comical pretender was Lambert Simnel, son of an Oxford tradesman, who in 1487 claimed to be Richard III's nephew and was actually crowned as Edward VI in Dublin. Manipulated by others who hoped to gain by making him king, he gathered an invading army which was defeated near Newark. Henry VII, realising that he was a dupe, pardoned him and gave him a job in the royal kitchens where he lived out an uneventful life.

Chariots of Ire
The revolting Boadicea

Boudicca was the wife of Prasutagus, ruler of the Iceni tribe of the area now known as East Anglia who had ruled as a nominally independent ally of Rome. He left his kingdom jointly to his daughters and the Roman Emperor but when he died his will was ignored and oppressive taxes were imposed on the Iceni. When Boudicca protested the Roman governor Paulinus had Boudicca flogged and her daughters were raped by Roman slaves. In AD 60, while Paulinus was leading a campaign in Anglesey, Boudicca led the Iceni in rebellion. They destroyed the Roman city of Camulodunum (Colchester) and routed a Roman legion which was sent to suppress the uprising. Londinium (London) and Verulamium (St Albans) swiftly followed, razed to the ground, with many thousands of Romano-British subjects perishing in the mayhem. Paulinus gathered his forces and overcame those of Boudicca in a battle which was known as the Battle of Watling Street and was probably

fought somewhere near Wroxeter in Shropshire. The crisis caused panic in Rome and prompted Nero to consider withdrawing all Roman forces from Britain but Paulinus's eventual victory over Boudicca secured the province for a further 300 years. Boudicca then died, possibly by her own hand. A persistent legend places her grave beneath platforms 9 and 10 of Kings Cross station in London. Her reputation underwent a revival during the 19th century when Queen Victoria was compared with her and statues were raised to her memory.

Medieval Myth or Real Romano-British Resistance Fighter?
King Arthur's Round Table

The legend of the Round Table dates from the 11th century when an Anglo-Norman poet called Wace, who was born in Jersey, suggested that King Arthur, the legendary Celtic warrior who supposedly resisted the Anglo-Saxon invaders before retreating to Cornwall and Wales, created a round table to prevent disputes amongst his knights over who should sit at the head of the table. The 'Round Table' in Winchester castle dates from about 1300 when the legend of Arthur was revived by Edward I and his sons. The date of the table was established by dendrochronology, or tree-ring dating, by comparing the timbers of the table with some taken from Nelson's flagship HMS *Victory* whose dates could be given with some confidence. A more recent suggestion is that the Round Table was in fact a reference to a Roman amphitheatre close to the Welsh border in Chester, a structure capable of holding 10,000 people where conferences could take place between a Celtic leader

and his followers. The legend of Arthur was given further impetus in the 15th century by Sir Thomas Malory, whose *Le Morte d'Arthur* was one of the first texts published by William Caxton. Malory, who died in 1471, is a mysterious figure who, though a Justice of the Peace, wrote the account of Arthur's deeds while in prison for rape, theft and violence. The legend underwent a further revival with the 19th century artists known as the Pre-Raphaelite Brotherhood, whose romantic images of Arthur and his companions are those which are most familiar. An iron age hill fort at Queen Camel in Somerset has as good a claim as anywhere to be the original Camelot but no table was found there when it was excavated in the 1960s.

Wessex Warrior
The life and times of Alfred the Great

Alfred, who reigned 871–99, is remembered for burning the cakes (for which there is no evidence, as they were eaten anyway) and for defeating the Danes. He certainly drove them from his kingdom of Wessex in a succession of savage battles but his achievement was not in fact to expel them but to confine them to the eastern half of England, which became known as the Danelaw, and to convert them to Christianity. Alfred united most of the rest of England under his rule by marrying the daughter of the king of Mercia, though England was not finally consolidated under one king until Alfred's grandson Athelstan (924–39). Alfred does however have a good claim to have founded the Royal Navy by creating a fleet designed to intercept Viking raiders. Above all he helped to shape the English language by sponsoring the Anglo-Saxon Chronicle. He is the only British king to be called 'the great'.

THE ANGLO-SAXON CHRONICLE
This early account of English history was begun in Alfred's reign, at his prompting, as an annual record of events to be kept in the Anglo-Saxon language, unlike previous chronicles which had been kept by monks like the Venerable Bede in

Latin. Alfred, and the **Anglo-Saxon Chronicle** *itself, therefore played a significant part in preserving the Anglo-Saxon tongue at a time when it was challenged by Danish and later by Norman invaders. It was compiled at major religious centres like Canterbury, York, Worcester and Abingdon from about 890 and continued to be kept at Peterborough as late as 1155, where it furnishes a lurid account of the chaotic reign of King Stephen. By 1155 the language had changed from Anglo-Saxon to something approaching the Middle English of Chaucer so it is a record of the development of English as a language as well an invaluable source of information on a turbulent phase of English history.*

The Importance of Being 'Unraed'
Aethelred and Canute in need of better advisers

A ethelred the Unready (968–1016) was king at a bad time in British history, as the Danes renewed their attacks on England in the century following the death of Alfred in 899. Ten years old when he became king, Aethelred had a very efficient system of tax collection which enabled him to pay Danegeld, in effect a bribe to deter the Danes from attacking his beleaguered kingdom. He had a bad press even among contemporaries, the *Anglo-Saxon Chronicle* criticising him for being indecisive – though the Anglo-Saxon word unraed which has become attached to his name actually meant 'ill-advised': that is, lacking good counsellors. At the time of Aethelred's death the Danish king Canute was invading England and eventually defeated Aethelred's son, Edmund Ironside, at Ashingdon near Southend in Essex. Edmund himself died in 1016 within a few months of his father. Like Aethelred, Canute (985–1035) has also been ill-served by historians. Having married Aethelred's widow Emma, Canute eventually became King of England and if, as is possible, he really did tell the advancing tide at Bosham in Sussex to turn back it was only to demonstrate to his flattering courtiers just how foolish they were to suggest that the tide would obey him.

Prince of Wales Bowled Out
Wayward Hanoverian son checks out in style

British novelist William Makepeace Thackeray (1811–1863) once quoted the following verse, author unknown.

> Here lies poor Fred who was alive and is dead,
> Had it been his father I had much rather,
> Had it been his sister nobody would have missed her,
> Had it been his brother, still better than another,
> Had it been the whole generation, so much better for the nation,
> But since it is Fred who was alive and is dead,
> There is no more to be said!

'Poor Fred' (1707–1751) was Frederick, Prince of Wales, eldest son of King George II, and a man who continued the Hanoverian tradition of sons quarrelling with fathers. George II objected to Frederick's extravagance and womanising;

Frederick occupied himself by running up debts, maintaining a separate court in opposition to his father on the present site of Leicester Square and to patronising, and occasionally playing, cricket. Cricket, however, was to be the death of him. He died of an abscess which arose from a blow to the head by a cricket ball in 1751. Since Frederick died before his father, Frederick's eldest son George III succeeded George II in 1760. Frederick was very popular in his lifetime and greatly mourned.

The Bard Comes Down Hard on the Thane of Glamis
Shakespeare's shortest tragedy: the Scottish Play

The Scottish king Macbeth, who reigned from 1040–1057, shares with Richard III the great misfortune of having had his character smeared by William Shakespeare. Shakespeare's demolition of Richard III was prompted by a desire to please Elizabeth I whose grandfather, Henry VII, had defeated Richard. Macbeth owed his misfortune to the legend that Banquo, whom Macbeth supposedly killed, was the ancestor of the Stuart dynasty and Shakespeare wished to please Banquo's descendant James I. By all accounts Macbeth was a man of charity who, when he visited Rome in 1050, 'scattered money like seed to the poor'. He lived at a bloodthirsty time when feuds and assassinations were a way of life in the fractured land which was less a unified kingdom than a collection of warring clans. As Shakespeare claimed, Macbeth did assassinate King Duncan and succeeded him in 1040 and was replaced by Duncan's son Malcolm in 1057. Nothing is known of his wife, the infamous Lady Macbeth. Although it is one of the shortest of Shakespeare's plays it is surrounded by more superstition than any of the others amongst actors who are themselves a superstitious tribe. It is regarded as unlucky to mention the name of the drama which is consequently routinely referred to as The Scottish Play.

Macbeth and Banquo meet the three witches. An illustration from Holinshed's Chronicles

Robert the Bruce Bides his Time
Destiny of Scotland not set in stone

Far more is known of Robert I – The Bruce – than of Macbeth. Edward I of England, having subdued Wales, turned his attention to Scotland and became known as the 'Hammer of the Scots', a phrase engraved in Latin (*Malleus Scotorum*) on his tomb in Westminster Abbey. Having failed to install a submissive candidate, John Balliol, as Scottish king, Edward removed from Scotland the Stone of Scone (also known as the 'Stone of Destiny') on which Scottish kings were traditionally crowned, took it south and had it incorporated into a specially designed Coronation Chair in Westminster Abbey. One legend claimed that the sandstone block had once belonged to the Old Testament prophet Jacob. An Irish origin is more likely. In the centuries that followed it featured in coronation ceremonies though it was damaged by suffragettes in 1914, and stolen and possibly broken by four Scottish students in 1950. It

was returned to Westminster for the coronation of Queen Elizabeth II and restored to Scotland in 1996 by the government of John Major.

Robert Bruce did not advance his claim to the Scottish throne until Edward I was ill in 1306 and Bruce took little part in the insurrections led by the Scottish hero William Wallace. Bruce was crowned Robert I in 1306 and Edward died the following year. Edward II waited until 1314 to attempt to assert his authority and suffered defeat at the Battle of Bannockburn, perhaps the most famous year in Scottish history. Robert succeeded in uniting his country against English threats and the Declaration of Arbroath in 1320 asserted the right of Scotland to exist as a separate kingdom, which it remained until the Scottish king James became sovereign of both countries in 1603.

The Guardian of Scotland
William Wallace – 'Braveheart'

While Robert Bruce bided his time and waited for the approaching death of Edward I, William Wallace had no such inhibitions. In 1297 he emerged from rather obscure origins as leader of the resistance to the English takeover of the Scottish kingdom when he won a notable victory over English forces at the Battle of Stirling Bridge. While many Scottish leaders made terms with the powerful English king, Wallace continued to lead the resistance but was defeated by a powerful English army, led by Edward I himself, at the battle of Falkirk in 1298. Wallace travelled to France to try to gain support from the French king, returning to Scotland in 1303 by which time Edward had succeeded in defeating or reaching terms with other Scottish leaders. In 1305 Wallace was captured, tried for treason (a trumped up charge since he had never owed allegiance to Edward) and executed at Smithfield in 1305 which now bears a monument to Wallace who has a claim to be the greatest of Scottish heroes. The 1995 film *Braveheart* suggested that Wallace fathered Edward II's son, the future Edward III. Since Edward II did not marry Queen Isabella until three years after Wallace's death this must be attributed solely to the imagination of the film's producer.

THE TARTAN KILT

The Scottish short or walking kilt (which was developed from a full length cloak) appeared in the 18th century. A letter to the **Edinburgh Review** *in 1785 suggested that it was introduced by an English Quaker called Thomas Rawlinson who supplied the garment to Scottish workers in his charcoal burning enterprise in northern Scotland and liked the garment so much that he wore it himself. In any case it became popular in the Highlands as a comfortable garment that was easy and cheap to make, but following the 1745 uprising led by Bonnie Prince Charlie all forms of Highland dress were banned except for Highland regiments serving in the British army. This ban was lifted in 1782 and the kilt, together with tartans for different clans, was re-introduced to the Lowland Scots when George IV visited Scotland in 1822, a visit whose pageantry was masterminded by Sir Walter Scott as an evocation of Scottish history.*

The Tragic Catholic Cousin of the Virgin Queen
Mary, Queen of Scots

Surely no queen led a more tragic life than Mary Stewart (1542–1587), queen of Scots from the age of six days to fifteen years. The name was conventionally spelt 'Stewart' until 1603 when her son became king of England and 'Stuart' thereafter. First betrothed to Henry VIII's son, later Edward VI, she moved at the age of 6 to France and married the Dauphin, the heir to the French throne, in 1558. The Dauphin died in 1560 and

in 1561 Mary, who had been brought up a Catholic at the French court, returned to Scotland, of which she had no memory from her infancy. There she found a firmly established Presbyterian church led by John Knox who cared neither for Catholics nor powerful women. Mary was descended from Henry VII through her father and in 1565 she married her cousin, Henry Darnley, who also had a claim to the English throne. The marriage was a disaster. It offended Elizabeth I of England who regarded the pair as potential claimants to her throne. Meanwhile Darnley's dissolute lifestyle caused the marriage to collapse. Darnley was murdered in 1567 by which time Mary had given

birth to their son, the future King James. A further unpopular marriage lost her what support she had in Scotland and led to her flight to England where her naïve complicity in plots to replace Elizabeth led to her execution in 1587.

KNOX'S MONSTROUS REGIMENT: HOW NOT TO CURRY FAVOUR WITH A QUEEN

In 1558, the year of Mary Stewart's marriage to the Dauphin and the first year of the reign of Elizabeth I, the Scottish Calvinist pastor, John Knox, published his pamphlet **The First Blast of the Trumpet Against the Monstrous Regiment of Women** *in which he declared 'how abominable before God is the Empire or Rule of a wicked woman, yea a traiteresse and bastard'. Knox had good reason to distrust women in authority. After capture by the French, in a conflict promoted by the French regent, Mary of Guise, Knox was made to work as a galley-slave, later escaping and living in England for a while. At the time that he wrote the pamphlet Knox was in Geneva,* *home of Calvinism. Elizabeth had just ascended the throne and was vulnerable to the claims of Mary Stewart. Moreover she had herself been denounced as a 'bastard' during the reign of her father Henry VIII following the execution of her mother Anne Boleyn for adultery. Knox had hoped that the Protestant Elizabeth would recall him from Geneva to a post in the English church. He explained to Elizabeth, 'I cannot deny the writing of a book against the usurped authority and unjust regiment of women; neither yet am I minded to retreat or call back any principal point or proposition of the same till truth and verity do further appear'. This was Knox's idea of an apology and it didn't impress Elizabeth. No recall followed. Knox's tact, diplomacy and timing were badly deficient.*

Placid Cymru?
Welsh princes: a quarrelsome lot

A ttempts to create a separate Welsh principality behind Offa's Dyke were frustrated by a mixture of English ruthlessness and inter-communal wrangling amongst Welsh princes. The first Welsh ruler to style himself Prince of Wales was Daffydd ap Llywelyn in 1244. He was recognized by the Pope and took advantage of the English king Henry III's quarrels with his nobles, notably Simon de Montfort. After Daffydd's death in 1246 his nephew, Llywelyn ap Gruffydd, married the daughter of Simon de Montfort and came close to establishing a united principality but made the mistake of alienating a number of other Welsh nobles, a number of influential church figures and, above all, Edward I of England who proceeded to invade Wales in 1276, leading to Llywelyn's death. The last serious attempt to create an independent Welsh nation was made by Owain Glyndwr who took advantage of the weakness of Henry IV of England who had deposed Richard II in 1399. Owain was supported by his kinsmen the Tudor family from Anglesey and further supported by Charles VI of France who was engaged in the Hundred Years' War with England and welcomed any activity which would inconvenience the English monarch. French support amounted to little and Glyndwr's rebellion petered out. He refused a pardon by Henry V in 1415 and died shortly afterwards. Within 70 years the Welsh Tudor dynasty were ruling England and there was little incentive for further rebellion.

William Conquers his Coronation Day Nerves
Beating the Christmas rush at Westminster Abbey

After his victory at the battle of Hastings William was crowned in Westminster Abbey on Christmas Day, 1066. Still nervous about the loyalty of his new Anglo-Saxon subjects, William posted a guard of Normans outside the Abbey to keep an eye on the crowd. Inside the abbey the assembled nobles were asked to acclaim the new monarch (as they still do in the coronation ceremony). This they did, loudly, in many dialects. Such was the noise that the Norman guards outside the abbey thought that William was being murdered so, to distract the supposedly treacherous throng, they proceeded to attack the

crowd and set fire to nearby buildings. In the words of a Norman chronicler, Orderic Vitalis, most of the nobles and the crowd 'made for the scene of conflagration, some to fight the flames and many others hoping to find loot for themselves in the general confusion'. The coronation of William as depicted on the Bayeux Tapestry shows none of these tumultuous events!

From Playboy Prince to Contemptible King
George IV: double-chinned son of a lunatic

Although he did not become king until 1820, George IV had acted as Prince Regent during the latter part of the reign of his father, George III, when the older man had suffered recurrent attacks of porphyria which rendered him mad. Father and son loathed each other, much of this arising from the Prince Regent's wanton extravagance on palaces, clothes and women. George spent a fortune on Carlton House as his London residence and then had it demolished when he moved to Buckingham Palace. He then spent a further £500,000 on his new home, leaving it an uninhabitable ruin at his death. A further £160,000 was spent on the domed splendour of Brighton Pavilion. In return for Parliament clearing his debts George agreed to marry his cousin, Caroline of Brunswick, in 1795 even though he had already contracted an illicit marriage to Anne Fitzherbert, a Roman Catholic. George and Caroline hated each other even more than father and son had done. They separated within a year. George resumed his many liaisons (including his marriage to Anne) and Caroline set off on a tour of Europe, shamelessly pursuing an affair with a young Italian servant. George tried to discredit Caroline by introducing a special Bill to Parliament but this was very unpopular with the public who cheered Caroline's appearances as they booed the Prince's. When George IV was crowned in July 1821 he ordered that Caroline be

Brighton Pavilion

excluded from Westminster Abbey and posted a guard to prevent her gaining entry. She became ill that day and died less than three weeks later. The coronation cost the equivalent of almost £20 million, 25 times as much as his father's had cost. It failed to make him popular. James Gillray drew a caricature of him as an obese 'voluptuary under the horrors of digestion' and when he died in 1830 *The Times* wrote: 'There never was an individual less regretted by his fellow-creatures than this deceased king. What eye has wept for him? What heart has heaved one throb of unmercenary sorrow? ... If he ever had a friend – a devoted friend in any rank of life – we protest that the name of him or her never reached us.'

Eminent Surgeons Save the Day with Acid, Scalpels and Cigars
World's first appendectomy a success for new king

E dward VII was almost sixty when he finally succeeded Queen Victoria in 1901, having spent his life in frustrated idleness. His mother seems never to have liked him very much and blamed him for the death of his father, Prince Albert, who had died, probably of typhoid, in 1861. Edward's appetites for food and women were legendary and when he was measured for his coronation robes his waist measured 48 inches (122cm). After much preparation the coronation was scheduled for 26th June 1902 and coronation medals, mugs and other souvenirs were produced bearing this date. Two days before the event, on 24th June, the king was struck down by appendicitis, a condition which at that time was usually fatal. Medical history was then made when a life-saving operation was performed by Sir Frederick Treves (1853–1923) and Lord Lister (1827–1912), the surgery taking place on a table in Buckingham Palace. Within a day the king was sitting up in bed smoking a cigar and from that time appendectomies became a regular medical procedure. The coronation duly took place six weeks later on 9th August 1902.

THE ELEPHANT MAN, CARBOLIC ACID AND RUBBER GLOVES
Sir Frederick Treves and Lord Lister were two of the most distinguished medical men of the 19th century. Sir Frederick Treves is mostly remembered for showing sympathy to the terribly deformed Joseph Merrick and for finding him a home in the London Hospital, Whitechapel, as featured in the 1980 film **The Elephant Man** *– though Treves's true distinction lay in his*

the French scientist Louis Pasteur (1822–1895) who had identified living organisms in the atmosphere and realized that these, later known as germs, could cause infection. Lister experimented with carbolic acid sprays in his operating theatres in the Royal Infirmary, Glasgow, and the death rate plunged. His theatre sister suffered from the effects of carbolic acid on her hands and this introduced the use of rubber gloves in the operating theatre.

achievements as a surgeon, notably in cases of appendicitis. Joseph, Lord Lister pioneered the use of carbolic acid as an antiseptic in operating theatres and thereby reduced the catastrophic mortality rates that had arisen following the introduction of anaesthetics in surgery earlier in the century. Although anaesthetics had eliminated the agonies of the operating table they also allowed surgeons to proceed more slowly, thereby exposing wounds to the dangers of infection for longer periods. In 1865 Lister read of the work of

Two Divorces, One Abdication and a Trip to See Hitler
The Scandals of Edward and Mrs Simpson

Following the death of George V in January 1936 his immensely popular son succeeded him as Edward VIII. But trouble was brewing and the old king had himself forecast that his son would reign for less than a year. After an unhappy childhood Edward, upon becoming Prince of Wales, had pursued a series of affairs with married women before becoming infatuated with Wallis Simpson, already divorced from an American and in a shaky marriage to her second husband, a British businessman called Ernest Simpson. Although the affair was widely publicized in the foreign press news of it was suppressed by British newspaper proprietors at a time when deference to royalty was the norm. In the autumn of 1936 Edward tried, with little success, to persuade the government of Stanley Baldwin that he could marry the now newly-divorced Wallis. He received little support, some of it coming from an embarrassing quarter: Oswald

Moseley's British Union of Fascists. On 1st December 1936 the Bishop of Bradford, Alfred Blunt, referred to the coronation ceremony as 'a solemn, sacramental rite'. Sections of the press seized upon this speech, interpreting it, quite wrongly, as a deliberate admonishment of the king's affair and the story broke with astonishing speed. On 10th December Edward abdicated and took the title of Duke of Windsor. He and Wallis married in France in 1937 and lived abroad for the rest of their lives, occasionally embarrassing their family and the British government, not least by visiting Hitler in October 1937 as war approached. Edward died in 1972 and his wife in 1986. They are buried side by side in the royal mausoleum at Frogmore, in the grounds of Windsor Castle.

'Who Will Rid Me of This Turbulent Priest?'
Henry II bashes a bishop in the name of the law

Henry II, who reigned from 1154–1189, is chiefly remembered for the murder of archbishop Thomas à Becket. Despite this blemish on his rule, he should rather be remembered as one of England's greatest kings and the creator of our system of justice. It was Henry's idea to send judges from Westminster to all parts of his kingdom to administer the king's justice at Assize Courts before returning to Westminster to compare notes with other judges. In this way a set of common principles was developed both in applying the law and determining sentences. This came to be known as the Common Law, the system which now applies throughout much of the world, including the Commonwealth and the United States.

Henry's problem was that a separate, and much milder system of justice, known as Canon Law, applied to offending clergymen, known as criminous clerks. Their cases were heard, and sentences determined, by bishops' courts, and a clergyman accused of a serious crime like murder or rape had a much better chance of escaping severe punishment in a bishop's court than a royal court. Moreover, since anyone with a rudimentary ability to read could claim the protection of the bishops' courts it meant that many who weren't ordained clergy could escape justice. The system deteriorated to a point where anyone who could read (or memorize) the opening words of Psalm 51 – 'Have mercy upon me O Lord according to Thy loving kindness' – was considered to be a candidate for trial in the bishops' courts. Becket resisted Henry's attempts to bring criminous clerks to justice within the royal courts, but this was forgotten when Becket was brutally murdered by some of Henry's knights in Canterbury Cathedral in late 1170. Canon law survived in a few matters into the 19th century. But Henry had a point!

Summary Execution, Cambridge University and Bloody Civil War
What did England's worst kings do for us?

King John and Henry VI are both strong contenders for the title of 'England's worst king'. Though innocent of persecuting Robin Hood, King John (reigned 1199–1216) was an oppressive king who deserved the uprising of nobles that led to Magna Carta. But one of his most inhumane acts led directly to the creation of Cambridge University.

St Edward, King and Martyr

In 1209 a young woman died in Oxford, possibly murdered by three students. We shall never know because King John ordered that they be hanged without a trial. In protest the authorities closed the university. Some of the more enterprising students made their way to a small market town in the East Anglian fens and thus Cambridge University was born.

Two and a half centuries later the devout Henry VI (reigned 1422–61 and 1470–71) decided to found a new college. Henry was concerned that Oxford had a reputation for heresy since John Wycliffe (1329–1384), Master of Balliol College, had studied the Bible and concluded that some of the church's doctrines were questionable. Henry was a deeply religious and orthodox man so he founded his new college, King's College, in Cambridge instead. To clear the site for his college he destroyed a church which was used by two existing colleges, Clare and Trinity Hall. To placate them, he granted the colleges the use of a nearby church called St Edward King and Martyr and, as a bonus, made it a Royal Peculiar which was outside the jurisdiction of the local bishop. Consequently it was possible to hold theological debates there without interference and in the following century it became a centre for discussion of the works of Martin Luther and thus the principal focus of heretical debate in England. Three of the leading 'Protestant' thinkers who debated there were Thomas Cranmer, Hugh Latimer and Nicholas Ridley who, in the reign of Queen Mary were burnt at the stake back in Oxford, where it had all started.

SCOT REWRITES ENGLISH HISTORY – AND BOTANY

The Wars of the Roses arose from the incapacity for kingship of Henry VI who at the age of nine months in 1422 succeeded his father, Henry V, the victor of Agincourt. However the expression 'Wars of the Roses' owes much more to literature than to history. The wars, fought intermittently between 1455 and 1485, were a struggle amongst the descendants of Edward III, who had died in 1377. One of these, Henry VI, was descended from the Plantagenet

Duke of Lancaster and another, Edward IV, was Duke of York and cousin to Henry VI. According to Shakespeare's play **Henry VI Part I**, *the opposing sides in the war gathered at the Temple church, in London, and declared their allegiance to one side or the other by plucking a white rose, to represent York, or a red rose to represent the claims of Lancaster. The two factions are represented by Richard Plantagenet, later Duke of York and John Beaufort, later Duke of Somerset:*

> *Plantagenet:*
> *Let him that is a true-born gentleman*
> *And stands upon the honour of his birth,*

The Tudor Rose

If he suppose that I have pleaded truth
From off this brier pluck a white rose with me.

Beaufort:
Let him that is no coward nor no flatterer,
But dare maintain the party of the truth,
Pluck a red rose from off this thorn with me.

There is no evidence that this event ever occurred, whether in the garden of the Temple church or elsewhere, but it was taken up by Sir Walter Scott in his now largely forgotten historical novel **Anne of Geierstein,** *or* **The Maiden of the Mist** *(1829) in which the expression Wars of the Roses was first used and from there it made its way into history books and legends. The roses were, however recognized as significant by the first Tudor king, Henry VII, a descendant of the Lancaster line, who ended the civil war by defeating the Yorkist Richard III at the battle of Bosworth in 1485. Henry married the daughter of Edward IV, Elizabeth of York,*

thus uniting the warring factions, and adopted as his heraldic symbol the Tudor Rose. This rose, unknown to botany, is a white rose set into a red rose. To this day, the sovereign is styled the Duke of Lancaster, regardless of gender.

Oliver Who?
The Welsh 'unknown' who won the Battle of Naseby

Fought in 1645 in Northamptonshire, Naseby was one of the critical battles of the English Civil War and destroyed the army of Charles I. The victory of the

Parliamentary forces was ensured by a decisive cavalry charge led by Oliver Williams. *Oliver Williams?* Yes, indeed. Thomas Cromwell (1485–1540) was Henry VIII's chief minister until he fell out with the king over Henry's disastrous marriage to Anne of Cleves. He was executed in 1540 but in the meantime had ensured that his family was well provided for. His elder sister had married a Welshman called Morgan Williams who came originally from Glamorgan but had set up business as an innkeeper in Putney. Thomas ensured that Morgan, and his son Richard, received substantial landholdings in Huntingdonshire which had been confiscated from Ramsey Abbey during the dissolution of the monasteries. Richard, out of gratitude to his uncle, changed his name to Cromwell and this was adopted by his son Henry and his grandson Oliver. Throughout his life Oliver Cromwell sometimes referred to himself as 'Oliver Williams alias Cromwell'.

A Grave End for Pocahontas
Native American princess unimpressed by Britain

Perhaps the most unexpected royal monument in Britain commemorates not a British monarch but a Native American princess. In the churchyard of St George's, Gravesend, is a monument to Pocahontas who died in 1617 and was buried nearby. Born in c.1595,

Pocahontas was the daughter of Emperor Powhatan who headed a group of tribes in the coastal region of Virginia which was settled by British colonists in 1607. John Smith, one of the colonists, was captured by some of the tribesmen after a dispute and was, he later claimed, rescued from execution by Pocahontas. During another dispute between the tribesmen and the settlers Pocahontas was captured and held for ransom during which time, in April 1614, she married an English tobacco farmer called John Rolfe. This appears to have improved relations between the two communities and in 1616 Pocahontas and Rolfe travelled to England to recruit more settlers for the colony. They lived for a while at Rolfe's ancestral home of Heacham Hall in Norfolk. Pocahontas was also presented at Court to James I and Queen Anne but, though treated with courtesy, was unimpressed by the scruffy and unprepossessing monarch. In March 1617 the pair boarded a ship to return to Virginia but Pocahontas became ill, possibly with smallpox, and died at Gravesend where she is buried. The couple had one child who has many descendants, amongst them two First Ladies: Edith Wilson, wife of the World War I President Woodrow Wilson; and, more recently, Nancy Reagan, wife of President Ronald Reagan.

BRITISH FOOD AND DRINK

Protein, Carbohydrate, Salt and Fat
Fish and Chips: Britain's culinary gift to the world

Fish and chips are first recorded as being offered by a Jewish fishmonger called Joseph Malin in the East End of London in 1860, though its origins as a meal lie much further back. Fried fish was a traditional Jewish dish which had been introduced to England when the Jews were invited back to England by Oliver Cromwell, after their expulsion by Edward I (who owed them money) in 1290. Chips probably originated in Belgium, the first reference to them in England being found in Charles Dickens's *A Tale of Two Cities* in 1859 where he refers to 'husky chips of potatoes, fried with some reluctant drops of oil'. The dish rapidly became a popular, cheap and nourishing food, and its popularity grew in World War II when it was one of the few foods that was not subject to any kind of rationing. The long tradition of eating them as a takeaway with salt and vinegar, wrapped in newspaper, was a casualty of the health alarms of the 1970s when it was suggested that the ink used on newspapers might be toxic but the food remains one of Britain's most popular dishes, with over 8,600 fish and chip shops in Great Britain. A variant of the traditional dish, fish fingers, were first produced in Grimsby in 1955 and remain extremely popular with children.

You Are What You Eat
Dieting to death: a Stark choice

In the 17th century scientists started to experiment to understand just what the British diet should be. One of the least successful but most heroic dietary experiments was conducted by a British doctor called William Stark (1740–1770) on himself. Stark was a friend of Benjamin Franklin who informed him that, in his younger days, he had lived on a diet of bread and water. Perhaps it was this that set Stark upon his fatal course. In June 1769, a healthy male weighing 12 stone 3 lbs, he started the diet by consuming nothing but bread and water for ten weeks. At the end of this time he had lost a stone in weight and his gums were swollen and bleeding, presumably from scurvy. He then adjusted the diet to consist of meat, milk and wine and then switched to bread, meat and water by which time he had 'blackened gums with foetid white stuff round their edges'. For a month he lived off 'puddings' consisting of flour, oils and water before deciding to adopt a new diet of fruit and vegetables. This would presumably have been his salvation since the diet would have provided the vitamins he needed. Unfortunately he changed his mind and confined himself to honey, puddings and Cheshire cheese. On 23rd January he died, racked with scurvy and a martyr to the cause of scientific enquiry. His last diary entry was 'Nothing passes through me except sometimes a little wind upwards or downwards and that without relief'. At no stage did he complain about his sufferings.

You've Never Had It So Good
Medieval peasant food

The medieval peasant diet in times of good harvests was one of the best we have ever enjoyed. This was pottage, a stew of fresh seasonal vegetables, pulses, cereals, seasoning and, when affordable, a little meat. This was supplemented by seasonal fruit, milk, cheese and bread baked from unrefined flour – that is to say flour containing most of the bran and other elements that are removed by the refining process which produces flour for white bread. This diet contained all the nutrients required for healthy, strenuous living centuries before anyone knew about protein, carbohydrate, fat, vitamins and minerals. It was very similar to the diet of the orphans of London's Foundling Hospital, founded in 1739 by Thomas Coram. This provided its charges with 'all the produce of the kitchen garden' – vegetables and fruit grown by the orphans themselves – as well as milk and meat.

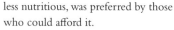

The Best Thing Since Sliced Flour and Water
The story of British bread

The Worshipful Company of Bakers is one of London's oldest Livery Companies, having paid a gold mark to the Exchequer every year since 1155. About 150 years later the bakers split into two factions which reflected later controversies about the nutritional value of bread that continued well into the 20th century. The bakers of brown bread formed their own guild producing a coarser (but more nutritious) bread from rye, barley or buckwheat (sometimes used in pancakes but not related to wheat at all). The bakers of white bread produced loaves from more refined wheat flour which, though

less nutritious, was preferred by those who could afford it.

In 1645 the two factions reunited into the Worshipful Company of Bakers which, even today, takes its place in the Lord Mayor's Procession and in the governance of the Square Mile. In 1266 the *Assize of Bread and Ale* was the first ordinance to set standards of quality, quantity and price. It laid down the relationship between the price of wheat and the farthing loaf which would be set annually by magistrates and 'four discreet men chosen and sworn thereunto'. Nine different kinds of bread could be baked, varying from superior Ranger Bread baked from white, sieved flour to Bread of Common Wheat which contained more roughage and, at half the price, was healthier. *The Liber Albus* ('White Book') compiled in 1419 at the request of Richard 'Dick' Whittington, Mayor of London, laid down the penalties to be imposed on bakers who produced defective bread (for example if the loaves contained sand):

> '... if any default shall be found in the bread of a baker of the City,

let him be drawn upon a hurdle from the Guildhall to his own house, through the great streets where there may be most people assembled, and through the great streets that are most dirty, with the faulty loaf hanging from his neck. If a second time he shall be found committing the same offence, let him be drawn from the Guildhall though the great street of Chepe, in manner aforesaid, to the pillory and remain there at least one hour.'

The pillory, in which the victim had to stand with his head and wrists held fast, could amount to a death sentence since onlookers were invited to throw anything to hand. Dead animals were favoured missiles and, though unpleasant, were rarely fatal but unpopular offenders could expect no mercy from a crowd which was usually drunk. One poor fellow, a counterfeiter, had his ears nailed to the pillory and only escaped by leaving parts of them behind.

Kaiser Bill and Hitler to the rescue of the British loaf

During the early modern period, an obstinate preference amongst the more affluent classes for refined white bread was applauded by many including Adam Smith who commented that 'the common people of Scotland who are fed with oatmeal bread are in general neither so strong nor so handsome as the same rank of people in England who are fed with wheaten bread'. He was misguided but his views were widely shared. During the 18th century poor harvests led Parliament to promote Standard Bread, marked with an S, costing less than white bread and containing more barley, oats and bran. It was healthier than refined white bread but regarded as inferior.

The controversy ran into the 20th century and was revived by Sir Oswald Mosley (1874–1928), father of the later Fascist leader, who persuaded Hovis to launch Smith's Old Patent Germ Bread whose nutritional qualities failed to overcome the familiar prejudice. It was soon withdrawn but the cause of nutritious bread was soon rescued by Kaiser Wilhelm II whose U-boats so curtailed the supply of wheat that British millers and bakers were obliged to reduce the amount of nourishing bran they removed from wheat in the refining process. In World War II an even less likely benefactor, Adolf Hitler, came to the rescue again when a shortage of wheat obliged a reluctant population to switch from white bread to the British Loaf which made a significant contribution to the wartime diet. After the war the conflict resumed between millers and nutritionists and it is only in the last thirty years that a large proportion of the British public has come to recognize that wholemeal bread is not only more nutritious: it also tastes better! The days when bread was the main element of our diet have long passed but we still consume, on average, about 720 grams per week, rather less than a loaf. If that seems a lot, just think of all those high-street sandwich shops.

Nice Cold Ice Cold Milk
Good for infants, depressed students and disease transmission

Milk has long been recognized as an exceptionally nutritious product and a staple of the British diet, though some of the ideas surrounding it have been bizarre in the extreme. In 1584 Thomas Cogan, the author of a book called *The Haven of Health*, explained that 'Milk is made of blood, twice concocted. Until it comes to the udder it is plain blood; but after by the proper nature of the udders it is turned into milk'. He added that it was recommended for those of a melancholy nature 'which is a common calamity of students'!

Cows in Soho and the black pump

As London's population grew, so did the demand for milk. In 1798 there were 8,500 cows in the city, many of them kept in squalid conditions, including basements in Golden Square, Soho. Dairymen would collect milk from the cows, add to it from the black pump (i.e. from water wells) and carry it in open buckets, where it was enriched by bird droppings, flakes of soot and general street dirt. But from 1840 the coming of the railways ensured a ready supply of fresh milk from the countryside, causing prices to fall and consumption to soar.

GOTTA LOTTA BOTTLE: THATCHER MILK SNATCHER!

In 1946 the Labour government of Clement Attlee introduced free milk for all schoolchildren. Those who attended school in the 1940s to 1960s can remember the special one-third-pint bottles which were dispensed during the morning break or dinner hour and consumed, sometimes reluctantly, under the eyes of the class teacher. They undoubtedly benefited many children, especially those from poorer families, but the free milk was withdrawn in the face of much criticism by the Education Secretary and future Prime Minister, Margaret Thatcher, in 1971. So before she became The Iron Lady she was known as Thatcher Milk Snatcher. Nowadays the average UK citizen consumes about 3 pints of milk per week, about 20 per cent above the average for Europe.

Taste the Difference: blonde or brunette?

In 1848 an article published in the respected medical journal *The Lancet* reported the results of some experiments carried out in France on breast milk. It claimed that 'in the milk of a brunette, when compared with that from females of fair complexion, there existed a greater amount of solid matter.' It added that 'milk is stated by some to be influenced greatly by mental emotions and even the sudden death of the infant has been asserted to have arisen from such alterations'. As far as is known neither of these propositions has subsequently been shown to be true.

Milk, among the most nutritious of natural products, was nonetheless associated with tuberculosis, the biggest cause of death in 19th century Britain. A survey of Manchester in the 1890s revealed that one fifth of the city's milk supplies was affected. A campaign to promote better hygiene in dairies followed and in 1901 Liverpool set up Infant Welfare Centres where sterilized milk was supplied, with immense benefits to the city's children. Other cities followed Liverpool's lead and these measures, together with the introduction of pasteurization (rapidly heating and cooling the milk to kill harmful microbes) meant that milk could much more safely be consumed.

'Wine is But Single Broth; Ale is Meat, Drink and Cloth'
The British love of good beer

It was Richard II who in 1393 decreed that all ale-houses should carry a distinctive sign so that they could easily be recognized by 'ale-conners' (those who tasted the ale for strength and purity). This accounts for the popularity of the number of 'White Hart' signs since this was the emblem of Richard himself. The importance attached to the quality of ale may be judged by the fact that it is mentioned in the *Magna Carta* and, along with bread, was the subject of the *Assize of Bread and Ale*

of 1266. The *Liber Albus* also describes processes by which the quality of ale was checked by elected officials. When a brewer 'shall have made a brew, send for the Ale-conners of the Ward wherein they dwell, to taste the ale, so that he or she sell no ale before that the said Ale-conners have assayed the same, under pain of forfeiture of the said ale.' If the ale was suspected of containing too much sugar then the test was to pour a pint on a wooden bench and sit on the damp patch in leather breeches until it was dry. If the breeches stuck to the bench the ale was over-sugared. Oddly, the use of hops in making beer was forbidden and in 1421 'information was laid against one for putting an unwholesome kind of weed called Hopp into his brewing'. Hops remained a prohibited ingredient until the reign of Edward VI after which the oast houses of Kent began to flourish. During the 19th century, when cholera and typhoid affected much of the water supply and caused many deaths, ale saved many lives as the brewing process kills harmful microbes.

WARM BEER

Britain's reputation for warm beer owes much to the difficulties of keeping draught beer cool and fresh in wooden barrels. In the 1970s major breweries attempted to overcome this problem by introducing keg beer, under pressure in metal containers, the beer itself often pasteurized. The resulting product, though cool, was often tasteless, one of the most notorious being Watneys Red Barrel. CAMRA (Campaign for Real Ale) was founded in protest and led to a revival of draught beer and the creation of hundreds of microbreweries serving local markets – though lager, a continental European creation, marches on relentlessly. Warm beer, however, survives in a few corners of the licensed trade despite the efforts of craft beers to eliminate it altogether!

The Water of Life
Whisky: the Celtic tipple of choice

James I's ancestor, King James IV of Scotland (reigned 1488–1513) liked a glass of whisky and granted the Edinburgh Guild of Surgeon Barbers the right to produce the drink in 1505 but it was James I himself, when king of England, who licensed the first distillery at Bushmills in Northern Ireland in 1608, where whiskey is still produced. The word derives from the Gaelic language (spoken in Ireland and Scotland), the original name being *usquebaugh*, meaning 'water of life'. Both Scotch whisky and Irish whiskey are produced mainly from malt and barley though the distillation process is slightly different. Early legends suggest that St Patrick learned the art of distillation on the continent (where it was certainly already in use) and took it to Ireland in the 5th century. There is more evidence to suggest that in the 6th century it was taken from Ireland to Scotland by the Dál Riata clan, overlords of the archipelagos and coasts of western Scotland and Northern Ireland. By the 17th century whisky was popular enough in Scotland for the Scottish Parliament to tax it and drive much of the production underground. In 1823 the Excise Act, passed by the British Parliament, moderated the taxes, licensed production and thereby created the foundations for what is now the worldwide whisky business. Scotch, with exports of over £4 billion a year, dominates as Scotland's largest export business.

Forget Toothpaste: Clean Your Teeth With Sugar
In defence of the sweet stuff

Most of us managed without sugar until well into the 16th century when its importation from India and the Americas found a ready market amongst the wealthier classes, human taste buds being predisposed to this sweet but nutritionally valueless product. Its cost meant that it could only be afforded by the wealthiest; this feature of the product was observed by a German visitor called Paul Hentzner who visited Queen Elizabeth I's court at Greenwich and commented: 'Her face oblong, fair but wrinkled, her eyes small yet black and pleasant, her nose a little hooked and her teeth black (a defect the English seem subject to from their too great use of sugar).' In the years that followed, a number of well-informed commentators observed the harmful effects of sugar, several of them commenting upon what later became know as tooth decay.

In spite of this, sugar found a redoubtable champion in Frederick Slare (1646–1727), contemporary and friend of Sir Isaac Newton and Fellow of the Royal Society whose book *A Vindication of Sugars* claimed that, far from damaging the teeth, he had 'made my Gums better and Teeth whiter' by rubbing them with sugar. Moreover, according to Slare his grandfather, who consumed prodigious quantities of sugar, grew to a hundred and had grown a fresh

set of teeth at the age of eighty! Slare also recommended it as a cure for sore eyes and scurvy. Annual sugar consumption peaked at about 43 kilos per head in the 1930s and, despite its well-known harmful properties the average British citizen still consumes approximately 37 kilos per year.

Mashed-up Organs Boiled in Guts, Anyone?
A natural history of the haggis

Haggis consists of sheep's offal (heart, liver and lungs) minced with onion, mixed with stock and simmered in the sheep's stomach for about three hours. It is traditionally served with 'neeps and tatties' (swedes, turnips and potatoes) boiled and mashed and with a 'dram' (glass) of Scotch whisky. The first recipe for 'hagese' is found in a book from

Lancashire dated 1430, a reference by the Scottish poet William Dunbar following in 1520. However, Robert Burns's 1787 poem, *Address to a Haggis*, has made it incontrovertibly Scotland's national dish and it is invariably served with great ceremony (and the poem recited) at the Burns Night supper celebrations which mark the poet's birthday on 25th January, an event celebrated not only in Scotland but throughout the world, notably in Russia.

Prostitutes Allegedly the Most Beautiful Women in Britain
In other news, potatoes cause leprosy

Potatoes, one of the great cornerstones of the modern British diet, did not arrive in Britain until the 1580s. Their introduction, from the Americas, is often attributed to Sir Walter Raleigh though the first reference to them by an Englishmen came from Sir Francis Drake. In November 1577, during his voyage round the world, Drake put into port in Chile and recorded that 'the people came down to us at the waterside with shew of great curtesie to bring us potatoes, rootes and two very fat sheepe'. The Germans erected a statue to Drake as the discoverer of the potato in the town of Offenburg but it was removed by the Nazis. In the early days it was a luxury product, two pounds of potatoes being supplied to Queen Elizabeth I for five shillings (25p) – far more than a working man's weekly wage at the time.

Spud-u-don't-like?
In the early days of the Royal Society scientists like Robert Boyle advocated the potato's cultivation while in his *Wealth of Nations* Adam

Raleigh

Smith commented that the product was popular amongst 'porters, coalheavers, prostitutes' and the Irish. He suggested that this explained why these groups were 'the strongest men and the most beautiful women in the British dominions'. The great economist also argued that if pasture and cornfields were turned over to the cultivation of potatoes then population would increase, profits would rise and prosperity would follow. Despite such champions the potato was slow to gain acceptance, one reason being the doctrine of signatures which prevailed in medical circles. This held that plants which resembled parts of the human body, especially when the body was diseased, were responsible for the

illness itself. The tubers of the potato were compared with the deformed hands and feet of lepers and the English writer Lovell, in his book *The Complete Herbal,* wrote of potatoes that 'if too frequently eaten they are thought to cause leprosie'. Not much of an endorsement there! During the World Wars the potato flourished as a year-round crop that was rich in nutrients and it was during World War II that a new strain was developed called Golden Wonder which later gave its name to a variety of potato crisp. £2 billion is now spent on potato based snacks every year, far more than is spent on potatoes in their raw state.

THE IRISH POTATO FAMINE

The Irish potato famine was a result of English exploitation and monoculture. It bedevilled Anglo-Irish relations. The green fields of Ireland had been used for centuries to pasture cows but as English and Scottish landlords used the grazing to feed the British taste for beef, Irish tenant farmers were forced on to poorer land where potatoes

were the most viable crop to feed a family. Potato blight arrived in Europe, probably from South America, in the early 1840s and was reported on the Isle of Wight in the summer of 1845. Its effects in England were damaging but, since potatoes were still a comparatively small element of the English diet, the effects were limited. By 1846 it had devastated the potato harvest in Ireland which, unlike England, was dependent on the crop to feed two thirds of its population. The reaction at Westminster, from which Ireland was ruled, was less than sympathetic. The normally benign Prime Minister Sir Robert Peel, commenting on the alarming reports from Ireland, wrote that there was 'always a tendency to exaggeration in Irish news'. Public works, such as constructing roads which even now lead nowhere, were an inadequate response to the tragedy as whole families died from starvation. Charles Trevelyan, the British Treasury official responsible for administering relief, declared that 'the judgement of God sent the calamity to teach the Irish a lesson, that calamity must

not be too much mitigated' though just what the 'lesson' was remains unclear. The immediate consequence of the famine was a great increase in emigration, especially to England and the United States. In the 1830s the Irish population had been 8 million. By the time the famine ended the population had fallen by half due to emigration and death from starvation. The population today is 6.6 million, 1.4 million less than it was almost two centuries ago. The famine gave additional impetus to the Irish independence movement.

Gathered By Virgins
The British love affair with tea

Tea reached Britain in the mid-17th century and is recorded as having been sold in a coffee house in Exchange Alley in London in 1657. Its proprietor, Thomas Garway, sold both liquid and dry tea, the latter at the extraordinary price of six pounds sterling per pound weight, claiming that it was 'gathered by virgins' and would 'make the body active and lusty', and 'preserve perfect health

Greenwich despite falling victim to a disastrous fire in 2007. Britons drink 165 million cups of tea each day, almost twice the 70 million cups of coffee which we consume.

Seeking a Healthy Balanced Diet? Go to War
Lake District ordeal for Nobel prize-winner

until extreme old age'. It vanquished nightmares, dispensed with the need for sleep and was especially recommended for corpulent men. It is hardly surprising that by 1750 tea had become Britain's favourite drink. An act of 1676 taxed tea and required coffee house operators to apply for a licence to sell it. By the middle of the 18th century the duty on tea exceeded 100 per cent. When the East India Company was given a monopoly on the tea trade in 1832, to bring the tea harvest to Britain they employed 'tea clippers' – streamlined, tall-masted vessels which could reach 18 knots, almost as fast as a modern ocean liner. The most famous surviving example is the *Cutty Sark*, built in 1868 and preserved at

It has been argued that the population of Great Britain was better fed during World War II than at any time before or since. Paradoxically this had a great deal to do with wartime shortages and rationing. Since much of Britain's food had to be imported across the dangerous Atlantic sea lanes it was essential to make maximum use of every nutrient. In December 1940 a group of scientists cycled from Cambridge to the Lake District and spent nine days trekking up and down mountains, carrying rucksacks filled with bricks that weighed 15 to 20 kg. They consumed only the amounts prescribed by the proposed wartime diet and assessed its effects on their

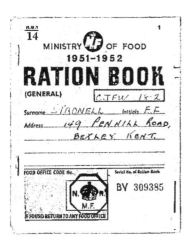

own wellbeing. Calorific intake and output were measured each day and the group concluded that the diet could be improved by such measures as adding calcium carbonate to bread and encouraging the consumption of wholemeal bread. The shortage of meat meant that the wartime diet was more vegetarian than normal but it delivered all the nutrients required and was later described by American commentators as 'one of the greatest demonstrations in public health administration the world has ever seen'. One of the intrepid band was (later Sir) Andrew Huxley, winner of the Nobel Prize for medicine and grandson of Thomas Henry Huxley, 'Darwin's Bulldog'. Another was Sir Jack Drummond who was killed in mysterious circumstances after the war.

MURDER IN PROVENCE

Sir Jack Drummond (1891–1952) was the leader of the group who developed the rationed wartime diet and a pioneer in the understanding and use of vitamins in the diet. He was also an enthusiastic traveller and camper. In August 1952 he travelled with his wife Anne and his ten year old daughter Elizabeth on a camping holiday to France. With the permission of the farmer, Gaston Dominici, they camped in a field near the small town of Peyruis in the valley of the Durance river, a remote and picturesque corner of France. The following morning they were all dead. The mother and father had been shot and Elizabeth's head had been smashed in by a rifle butt which had broken off under the force used to kill the child. Elizabeth's body was almost 100 yards away from those of her parents, across a bridge, suggesting that she had witnessed the murder of her parents and tried to flee. Gaston Dominici was convicted of the murders in November 1954 and sentenced to be guillotined. Doubts about the police investigation and the trial led President Rene Coty to commute the sentence to life imprisonment. His successor, General de Gaulle, released Dominici on humanitarian grounds without a pardon. The motive for the murders remains a mystery.

Marmite for the Masses!
The National Birthday Trust Fund

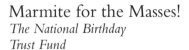

In the decade before World War II the National Birthday Trust Fund sought to improve the diets and consequently the health of pregnant women from poorer areas. It was the brainchild of the wealthy Marchioness of Londonderry whose Park Lane mansion (demolished in 1965 to make way for the Hilton hotel) was an unusual gathering place for an organization devoted to supporting malnourished pregnant women. The idea was to collect a shilling (5p) from all citizens on their birthdays, giving a total of over 40 million shillings, or £2 million, to feed the poor. Hardly any of the army of 3 million unemployed, or their families, could afford a shilling for anything but enough money was raised to distribute jars of vitamin-rich Marmite, beef drinks, Ovaltine and milk-based drinks to distressed and vulnerable folk in areas like South Wales, resulting in a marked fall in infant mortality. The spirit of this charitable venture was compromised by the event held to mark its success. On 28th March 1939 a lavish dinner was held at the Guildhall, London, attended by the Queen and many society ladies. Two hundred women who had benefited from the scheme were bussed in as exhibits but they were not amongst the dinner guests. Each was provided with a ninepenny (4p) luncheon box from Lyons while the celebratory feast proceeded out of their sight.

BEANZ MEANZ JARZ

Baked beans (in fact they are normally stewed rather than baked) were introduced to the British public in the fashionable Fortnum and Mason shop in Piccadilly in 1886 and marketed as an expensive and exotic import from the USA. They are mostly made from haricot beans, also called navy beans, which are native to North America but have been cultivated on a small scale in

Britain. They are Britain's favourite tinned product, especially amongst children, with the contents of 1.5 million tins being consumed each day, most of them made by Heinz. The people of Trafford in Manchester consume over half a million tins per year, more tins per head than anyone else and enough to bury Manchester United's nearby football pitch four times over. They are a healthy product, containing both vitamins and 'roughage', the latter accounting for their well-known side-effect as bacteria get to work on them in the gut. In 2010 they were for the first time sold in jars which can be resealed and returned to the refrigerator.

Disease and Death in the Pot and Bottle
Detecting fraudulent and deleterious adulterations

In January 1831 *The Lancet* reviewed a book whose title tells its readers all they need to know about its contents. The book was called *Deadly Adulterations and Slow Poisoning, or Disease and Death in the Pot and Bottle*; *in which the Blood-empoisoning and Life-Destroying Adulterations of Spirits, Beer, Bread, Flour, Tea, Sugar, Spices,*

Cheesemongery, Pastry, Confectionary, Medicines etc. are laid open to the Public, with Tests and Methods for ascertaining and detecting the Fraudulent and Deleterious Adulterations and the good and bad Qualities of those Articles: with an Expose of Medical Empiricism and Imposture, Quacks and Quackery, Regular and Irregular, Legitimate and Illegitimate; and the Frauds and Malpractices of Pawnbrokers and Alehouse Keepers. By an Enemy of Fraud and Villainy, 1830.

For the purposes of publication, both the author of the book and its reviewer were anonymous though the reviewer was probably the editor of The Lancet, Thomas Wakley, who founded the journal to campaign against quack medicines and the widespread adulteration of food. Wakley followed up the review by commissioning his own enquiries in the years that followed and publishing the findings in his home-grown organ.

Always read the label

Peruvian bark, sold as a remedy against malaria, was often in reality mere sawdust from English oak, a quarter the price of the genuine article to the chemist (though not, of course, to the unwitting customer).

Tea was found to contain elder, ash, molasses and clay, with liquorice being added to impart colour to tea leaves which had already been used. Another trick was to collect used tea leaves and coffee grounds from London hotels, boil them with ferrous sulphate and sheep's dung and restore their colour with verdigris or carbon black before reselling them.

Green pickles were more expensive than brown and the desired coloured effect could be achieved by boiling brown pickles in a copper vessel with

copper coins. Even this abomination, however, was less harmful than the method for clarifying cloudy white wine which required the 'wine merchant' to put melted lead into the cask and seal it for a while. Red wine, on the other hand, could be made redder by adding potash! Likewise black pepper could be converted into the more expensive white pepper by steeping the black pepper in a mixture of sea water and urine (human or animal).

Milk was found by *The Lancet* to have been diluted with water which was itself often foul but more alarmingly some dairies offset the effects of the water by adding snails to the mixture, their mucus acting as a thickening agent while producing a pleasant and reassuring froth on the surface of the liquid. Red lead and arsenite of copper were used to give colour to cheese while sulphuric acid and powdered glass imparted smell and texture to foods and snuff. Sugar contained large quantities of wood, lime, iron and, more worryingly, living insects and lead. Since lead was expensive as well as poisonous it must be assumed that this, along with other foreign substances, had probably entered the food chain by accident rather than by design.

Coffee and chocolate houses had been expensive and fashionable gathering places since the middle of the 17th century and they feature in the diary of Samuel Pepys at that time. Since the products they sold were also expensive they began to attract the attentions of the most skilled chemical forgers who added roasted peas and beans, butter, dandelion, parsnip and, surprisingly, lard to bulk up the products. Contemporary writers even advised different adulterating substances for different markets: 'the other ingredients for making chocolate may be varied according to the constitutions of those who are to drink it.' Nutmegs, clover and lemon peel were advised for those with 'cold constitutions' while for those of warmer temperaments almonds and rhubarb were preferred, the rhubarb alone being added for 'young green ladies', whatever they were. Our ancestors must have had cast-iron constitutions to survive all that!

Champagne: made in Britain!
But called 'fizzy wine' for copyright reasons

In December 1662 Dr Christopher Merrett (1615–1695), a physician from Gloucestershire, presented a paper to the recently formed Royal Society called S*ome Observations concerning the ordering of wines.* He described a process by which sugar and molasses could be added to wine to induce a secondary fermentation in the bottle and make sparkling wine. Merrett's interest appears to have lain more in the process by which glass bottles could be made strong enough to accommodate the fermentation without exploding, a technique pioneered by Sir Robert Mansell in Newcastle earlier in the 17th century. So the British had the fermentation

techniques and the bottles to produce wine by the *methode champenoise* long before Dom Perignon in 1697. Unfortunately they didn't have the grapes! Merrett's name is sometimes used on bottles of British sparkling wines. Britain, which had many vineyards run by monasteries before their dissolution by Henry VIII in 1535, is undergoing a revival in its viticulture. There are now 500 vineyards in England and Wales, some of them producing high quality white wines without the adulteration so commonplace in previous centuries.

Mother Nature's Bountiful Harvest
The ripe realities of early recycling

Given the prevalence of dangerously adulterated foods a vegetarian diet might have been advisable, using only produce direct from the ground – but even that would have had its pungent dangers. In his account of *Six Weeks Tour Through the Southern Counties of England and Wales*, published in 1771, Arthur Young commented approvingly on the fact that fresh

vegetables were being conveyed cheaply to the markets of London and other towns and cities via the developing system of canals; but Young then noted, equally approvingly, that on the journey to the farms to collect the vegetables, the barges would have carried cargoes of human excrement from the towns to manure the fields in a virtuous cycle of recycling!

MASTICATING IS GOOD FOR YOU

The pre-eminent Victorian Prime Minister William Gladstone (1809–1898) was a believer in the practice of chewing food thirty-two times (once for each tooth) before swallowing it, believing that this would make better use of the food and thus enable him to survive on smaller quantities. This idea became known as 'Fletcherism' when it was adopted by an American called Horace Fletcher (1849–1919) – nicknamed 'The Great Masticator' – and was taken up by Kennedy Jones (1865–1921), the co-founder of the Daily Mail. Jones became director of food economy at a time of food shortage during World War I. He used his contacts amongst journalists to publicize the notion that less food would need to be brought across the perilous Atlantic shipping lanes if only people could be persuaded to masticate more thoroughly. His arguments were ridiculed by the scientists of the Royal Society and Kennedy Jones's well-meaning contribution to the war effort ended in ignominy shortly afterwards.

'A thousand screaming victims'

The Vegetarian Society was formed at Ramsgate in Kent in 1847 by Joseph Brotherton MP (1783–1857) and his wife whose contribution was to write early vegetarian cookbooks which substituted loaves and melons for the loaves and fishes of the Biblical miracle. In Britain the most conspicuous vegetarian was the playwright George Bernard Shaw whose vegetarian zeal was compromised by the wife of the artist William Morris who surreptitiously fed him pudding containing suet. However Brotherton was not the first or most fanatical British vegetarian, a prize that could be claimed by the poet Percy Bysshe Shelley (1792–1822). In 1812 Shelley wrote *A Vindication of Natural Diet* in which he attributed many of the world's ills to the practice of consuming meat:

> 'Hospitals are filled with a thousand screaming victims; the palaces of luxury and the hovels of indigence resound alike with the bitter wailings of disease; idiotism and madness grin and rave among us and all these complicated calamities result from the unnatural habits of life to which the human race has addicted itself during innumerable ages of mistake and misery.'

He went on to compare the vicious habits of carnivorous humans with the gentle, vegetarian orang-utan. He advised his readers, in capital letters: 'NEVER TAKE ANYTHING INTO THE STOMACH THAT ONCE HAD LIFE'. Having deserted his young wife, who drowned herself in the Serpentine, he was himself drowned in Italy at the age of thirty. His death was celebrated in some circles, mourned in others.

17TH CENTURY BATTERIES

Battery hens are not new. In the middle of the 17th century Sir Kenelm Digby (1603–1665) wrote a report on a visit to a chicken farm. Digby's father had been executed for his part in the Gunpowder Plot of 1605 but despite this the son gained favour with James I and Charles I and enjoyed a successful career as a privateer (a licensed pirate preying on French and Spanish ships). As the

owner of a glassworks he is credited with inventing the modern wine bottle design. He wrote extensively on food and agriculture and his comments on three features of the farm he visited are worth recalling. First, the chickens were fed a mixture of barley and milk because this had been shown to make them grow more rapidly than barley alone. Secondly, they were confined in small coops so that they could not move around, this lack of exercise ensuring that they did not lose the weight they had gained. Finally, a candle was left burning in their coops at night to keep them awake and, it was hoped, feeding. Such conditions would be recognized by a modern battery hen.

wife of Oliver Cromwell, had a reputation as a fine cook with a nose for a bargain. During the period that Joan's husband was Lord Protector a countrywoman brought a bag of peas to London, the first peas of the season, and turned down the substantial sum of five shillings offered by a cook in the Strand (close to the present site of the Savoy Hotel) in the hope of obtaining a better price from Joan Cromwell. She was disappointed, being offered only half the sum by the thrifty Joan whose husband would no doubt have disapproved of any unpuritanical extravagance.

Keeping Up with the Cromwells
Mrs C: a fine cook and a better haggler

In the 17th century the ability amongst prosperous citizens to be able to serve seasonal foods before one's neighbours was a sign that one was well-connected. Joan Cromwell,

Britannia Rules the Waves Thanks to Pickled Cabbage
Scurvy and the French Navy defeated by British grocers

The efficient prevention of disease and the provision of nutrition to hard-toiling naval crews occupied many leading minds in the 17th and 18th centuries. In both fields the

British Admiralty could call on truly groundbreaking pioneers whose unglamorous but vital contribution to British naval mastery is difficult to overstate. Portable soup was invented in the 18th century as a means of victualling the ships of the Royal Navy on long voyages. A recipe for it was included in *The Art of Cookery* in 1747. A broth of lean meat was created, the fat having been removed to prevent rancidity. Bones and vegetables would be added, together with salt to act as a preservative. The mixture would be repeatedly boiled and strained for hours until it had the constituency of jelly which would be cut into slabs. These could be reconstituted by immersion in hot water and provided a palatable meal, though lacking in vitamins. Portable soup was routinely carried in Royal Navy ships from about 1750, including those of Captain Cook in his explorations of the South Seas.

However the most beneficial product that Cook carried was undoubtedly pickled cabbage, also known as sauerkraut. The great scourge of the seamen of the 18th century and earlier was scurvy,

HMS Endeavour

symptoms of which were described by a naval doctor of the time:

'Swelled legs, putrid gums, extraordinary lassitude of the whole body, ulcers of the worst kind, attended with rotten bones and a luxuriancy of fungous flesh as yielded to no remedy.'

Although the existence of vitamin C and its antiscorbutic role in preventing scurvy was not understood at the time, several seafarers had noted that consumption of certain products such as citrus fruits and pickled cabbage appeared to prevent or cure the condition. When Cook set off on his first voyage in 1768 on HMS *Endeavour* it was victualled with sauerkraut. The seamen did not care for the sauerkraut so he resorted to psychology to overcome their aversion:

> 'I had some of it dressed every day for the officers' cabin table and left it to the option of the men to take as much as they pleased or none at all...before a week I found it necessary to put everyone on board to an allowance.'

On his return Cook gave an account of his voyages to the Royal Society whose future President, Sir Joseph Banks (1743–1820) had accompanied Cook. He reported that 'Sour Kraut, of which we had a large provision, is not only a wholesome vegetable food but, in my judgement, highly antiscorbutic and spoils not by keeping.' For his account Cook was awarded the Royal Society's Copley Medal, its highest accolade, later awarded to Charles Darwin and Albert Einstein. From that time seamen of the Royal Navy were less vulnerable to scurvy than were those of other navies, which gave the fleets of Nelson and others a great strategic advantage in protecting British shipping and the expansion of British trading networks in what was an era of growing worldwide empire of colonies and commercial hubs. Nelson's fleet which blockaded French ports before Trafalgar carried 30,000 gallons of citrus juice to enable sailors to remain at sea without developing symptoms of scurvy.

DAMN LIMEYS

The expression 'Limeys' became current in America during the 19th century to refer to British sailors and, by extension, to Britons in general because of the practice of supplying Royal Navy and merchant ships with lime juice to ward off scurvy. It originally had a slightly ironic meaning because Americans couldn't understand this strange practice but as the benefits of citrus juice were demonstrated it almost became a term of affection.

BRITISH GOVERNMENT: POLITICS, MONEY AND THE LAW

Tories and Whigs
Bandits and covenanters

'Tories and Whigs' were expressions which developed during the late17th century to describe political opponents. Neither was complimentary. The word 'Tory' was derived from an Irish expression meaning a bandit or outlaw and referred to those who were sympathetic to the legitimate claims of the catholic James, Duke of York to succeed his brother Charles II as king. The word 'Whig' was derived from a Scottish expression 'whiggamore', which had been used to describe Scottish covenanters who in the reign of Charles I had defended the rights of the Scottish Presbyterian church against the attempts by Archbishop Laud to reform their practices and bring them into line with those of the Anglican church. Over the following three centuries the term 'Tory' came to be associated with the Conservative party and 'Whig' was attached to the Liberal Party, particularly to its wealthy landowning supporters.

Speak Up Mr Speaker!
The historical reluctance to answer back

Why is the Speaker of the House of Commons (and of many other legislative assemblies including the US House of Representatives) called 'Mr Speaker' or 'The Speaker' when he doesn't speak in debates? And why, when he or she is elected to the post, does the candidate have to be dragged, 'protesting' to the Speaker's chair?

The answers may be found in the behaviour of the first recorded holder of the post. This was Sir Peter de la Mare who, before entering Parliament, had been Sheriff of Herefordshire. The Good Parliament of 1376 instituted proceedings against some of the advisers of Edward III who was ailing, shortly to die and unduly influenced by corrupt courtiers. Peter de la Mare, having presided over the debate that led to the indictments, then had to communicate the decisions of the Commons to the king's son, John of Gaunt, thereby acting as 'Spokesman' or 'Speaker' on their behalf. John of Gaunt was furious and had de la Mare arrested and imprisoned. He was later released and compensated by Richard II when he ascended the throne the following year in 1377 but de la Mare's ordeal illustrated the perils that could arise from carrying unpopular messages to a powerful king. Hence the need to drag him or her to the chair.

'AYES' AND 'NOES' YOUR MAJESTY

When a vote is taken in the House of Commons this is done by asking MPs to walk through the 'ayes' (in favour) or 'noes' (against) lobby in the House. This is known as a 'Division' because the MPs divide as they approach the lobbies. In medieval Parliaments there was no formal division. A debate would be held and the Speaker would then have the sometimes hazardous task of conveying the sense of the debate to the king. The first Parliamentary Division occurred during the reign of Henry VIII when the House of Commons was debating the king's request for taxes. Fearing an unfavourable outcome Henry insisted that the house divide, those favouring his request going to one end of the chamber and those opposing it to the other, while he watched. The king, unsurprisingly, got his taxes from this, the first Parliamentary Division!

'I have neither eyes to see nor tongue to speak'

A critical incident occurred in January 1642 when King Charles I, enraged by the refusal of Parliament to allow him to raise taxes without its authority, entered the House of Commons to arrest five members who had been his most resolute opponents. They had made good their escape. The king commented 'the birds have flown' and when the king asked the Speaker, William Lenthall, where they were, Lenthall famously replied: 'May it please your Majesty, I have neither eyes to see nor tongue to speak in this place but as the House is pleased to direct me, whose servant I am here.' From that day no monarch has entered the House of Commons. When the Queen opens Parliament

she sends her messenger, Black Rod, to summon the Commons to attend her in the House of Lords. As Black Rod approaches the House of Commons the door is slammed in his face as an assertion of the House's authority. When they obey his summons the MPs walk slowly and casually to the Lords, chatting amongst themselves to indicate that they are obeying the summons by choice rather than compulsion of the monarch.

The King's Jews
William the Conqueror's heritage and the Jewish community in Britain

There is some evidence for the existence of a Jewish community in Britain before 1066 (apart from the legend that Joseph of Arimathea brought Jesus to England and established a religious community on Glastonbury Tor). For instance there is a record from the time of Edward the Confessor which states that 'the Jews and all theirs belong to the King'. William the Conqueror certainly encouraged Jews from

William I

Rouen in France to settle in England. It has even been suggested that William's mother Arlette (also known as Herleva), a tanner's daughter who was seduced by William's father Duke Robert, was herself of Jewish ancestry. From the time of William, the Jewish community was known as 'the King's Jews' and had to reside in places specified by the monarch. For two centuries their affairs were supervised by a special department of government, the Exchequer of the Jews, whose main concern was to ensure the welfare of the community and its availability as a source of finance. For a Jewish community had one major advantage for a medieval king: money. The prohibition on

usury (i.e. loans for interest, or banking) by the medieval church did not apply to Jews who were thus able to enjoy a virtual monopoly of this profitable activity.

THE PAWNBROKERS OF LOMBARD STREET

The Lombards, from the region around Milan in northern Italy, circumvented the laws against usury by setting up as pawnbrokers: lending money against the security of a valuable item and then returning it to the owner for more than originally advanced. This was an early form of banking and many of them set up businesses in the City of London in the area now known as Lombard Street – still the headquarters of many banks.

The unpopularity as well as the prosperity of many Jews made them a fertile source of money, extracted not just through taxes. In 1177 Jurnet the Jew was fined the unimaginable sum of £1,333 at Winchester for crossing the channel without the king's permission. Moreover when a Jew died the king received a third of his estate. In 1186 when Aaron of Lincoln died Henry II received so much (over £15,000) that he set up a special department, the Exchequer of Aaron, with four full-time staff to administer it. The Jewish community remained until 1290, their blameless lives occasionally punctuated by massacres. In that year Edward I imposed a tallage of £12,000 on the Jews. A tallage was a tax imposed by the king on his own property and, as we have seen, Jews were regarded as belonging to the king. The tallage raised £4,000 so Edward, dissatisfied with this sum, ordered their expulsion. Sheriffs were ordered to ensure safe conduct for the Jews to London from where they were sent to the continent. It had the convenient effect, for the king, of cancelling the debts he already owed to them.

They were invited back by Oliver Cromwell in the 1650s and their financial acumen was of importance in promoting British trade from that time onwards. In the meantime other means had to be found of raising money for the royal exchequer. One of these was the Poll Tax.

The Poll Tax
Ignore history at your peril

The 'Poll Tax Riots' of 1990 which precipitated Margaret Thatcher's fall from power had a precedent in the Peasants' Revolt of 1381, led by Jack Straw, Wat Tyler and the priest John Ball. Our medieval ancestors were much more patient over this burdensome taxation than the rioters of 1990 since they only rebelled against the *third* attempt to tax them. The first poll tax was levied in 1377 by the government of Richard II who was then only ten years old, having succeeded his grandfather, Edward III, the same year. Richard's father, the Black Prince, had died the previous year after campaigning in France and the tax was necessary because of the cost of waging the war in pursuit of Edward III's claim to the French throne. This was the conflict that was to become the Hundred Years' War. This first poll tax was a flat rate tax of 4d (about 1.6p) on every person aged 14 or over except clergy who paid a shilling (5p). Richard's uncle, John of Gaunt, whose London home was the Savoy Palace in the Strand, then launched a futile attack on the French port of St Malo which incurred further expense and necessitated a second poll tax in 1379. For this second poll tax the rate varied from 4d for the poorer citizens to two shillings (10p) for the more prosperous and as much as £4 for the nobility, though the clergy were exempt from this second tax. The amount raised still proved inadequate to pay off the English troops in France before they deserted so a third poll tax was levied in 1381.

It was this third poll tax of 1381, again levied at a flat rate for everyone of three groats (one shilling, or 5p), that provoked the uprising which began in Essex and Kent. The king's tax collectors were attacked, the Archbishop of Canterbury was beheaded and the Savoy Palace of John of Gaunt, whose failed raid on St Malo in Brittany had created the need for the tax, was sacked. Richard II, now 14, agreed to meet the rebels at Smithfield where the Mayor of London, William Walworth, stabbed Wat Tyler and the revolt fizzled out. Richard II did not live up to his early

---

WHY 'GAUNT'?

John of Gaunt, founder of the House of Lancaster which eventually triumphed in the Wars of the Roses, owes his name to the fact that he was born in the town of Ghent, now in Belgium, and which was anglicized to Gaunt.

---

promise. He became increasingly unpopular throughout his reign and was eventually deposed by his cousin, John of Gaunt's son, who became Henry IV in 1399. In 1641 Charles I, a monarch even more unpopular than Richard II, tried to introduce a poll tax. This was one of the events that sharpened his conflict with Parliament and helped to precipitate the Civil Wars which resulted in his death. So poll taxes do not have a good record and Mrs Thatcher, if she had known her history, might have thought better of her poll tax or 'community charge' as she preferred to call it. But then she was a chemist by training, not a historian.

Father of English Literature Swaps Quill for Shears
Chaucer's woolly stock-in-trade

In 1374 Geoffrey Chaucer, poet, philosopher, courtier and author of *The Canterbury Tales*, was appointed by Edward III as Controller of the Customs for hides, skins and wool in the port of London. During the latter part of the 14th century exports

of woollen cloth from England increased almost tenfold. Earlier in the century the crown had agreed that Parliament should have the right to be consulted on measures of taxation. In return Parliament had granted the wool subsidy, a measure by which a customs duty was levied on exports of English wool. The revenue from this trade accounted for between half and two thirds of royal revenue in Chaucer's time. The tax on exports was attractive because it was easy to administer and the demand for English wool in the later middle ages was so great that the trade could bear it. However as it became evident that it wasn't exactly a trade promotion measure other methods had to be found.

Morton's Fork
The crafty cardinal and the lost monasteries

John Morton (1420–1500), who judiciously changed sides during the Wars of the Roses, became Archbishop of Canterbury in 1486 and Henry VII's Lord Chancellor the following year. Francis Bacon (1561–1626), who was one of his successors as Lord Chancellor, left an account of Morton's tax-raising methods which passed into history as 'Morton's Fork'. According to Bacon, when Morton visited one of the king's subjects and was lavishly entertained he would conclude that the host was well-placed to make a generous tax payment or loan to the king; and when Morton was thriftily entertained he

would arrive at the same conclusion by declaring that the host's modest lifestyle must have enabled him to accumulate a large fortune. Whatever the truth of Bacon's claim, Henry VII's ability to raise taxes and keep the royal finances in good shape was legendary and owed a good deal to his Lord Chancellor for whom he secured a Cardinal's hat in 1493. In the following reign Henry VIII, a more extravagant monarch than his father, filled the royal coffers by dissolving the monasteries and confiscating their wealth.

Stamping Out the Smugglers
British efforts to prevent trade in untaxable contraband

In the 18th century the costly wars with France led the government to try to raise money by taxes on imports of products like brandy, wine, tobacco and above all the increasingly popular tea. Unfortunately for the government these were all high-value low-

volume products which were easy to smuggle and the taxes spawned a huge alternative economy, especially around the south-east coasts of Britain which faced the continent. Large contingents of customs men fought gangs of smugglers who were so numerous and well-organized that they amounted to well-financed small armies. The most notorious was the Hawkhurst Gang which, from 1735–49, operated from the village of Hawkhurst in Kent, conveniently close to the flat coastline of Romney Marsh which was a favoured landing for smugglers. The gang was put out of business when its two leaders, Arthur Gray and Thomas Kingsmill, were hanged in 1748 and 1749. Others replaced them and they were merciless in their dealings with the customs men who hunted them. One customs officer who was captured by brandy smugglers was forced to drink as much brandy as he could before passing out, whereupon a further two and a quarter pints were poured down a funnel into his mouth, after which he was tied to a horse and set loose. The smugglers' trade was eventually ended by two developments. First, the

chain of Martello Towers constructed to oppose Revolutionary and Napoleonic French landings provided convenient bases for the national coast guard which was established in 1824.

MARTELLO TOWERS

In 1794, during the wars against France, the Royal Navy with great difficulty captured a small fortification at Cape Martella in Corsica. Impressed by its simple but effective design, the British government built a chain of 103 similar forts around the south-east coast of England from Suffolk to Sussex to resist a potential invasion by Napoleon. They were built of brick, 13 feet thick on the seaward side to withstand bombardment, less sturdy on the landward side, with a garrison of one officer and 24 men to

man one gun in each Martello Tower.
Oval in shape, they were designed
so that most cannon balls would be
deflected away. They were never tested
in war. More than forty of them
survive, some having been converted
to dwellings.

An even more decisive step against smuggling had been taken forty years earlier, in 1784, when the East India Company persuaded the government to reduce the duties on tea to a point where the smugglers had little to gain. In two years the legitimate imports of tea grew from 5.8 million to 16.3 million pounds weight, which gives some idea of the quantity that was previously being smuggled. In the following century other tariffs were reduced or abolished as Britain entered its era of Free Trade. In 1815 the government passed the Corn Laws. This was a form of excise tax on wheat, the purpose of which was to protect British farmers against cheaper imported produce rather than to raise money for the government. Since wheat was a bulky product it was much more difficult to smuggle than tea, tobacco and alcohol.

The Corn Laws were unpopular because they forced up the price of bread and made only a very small contribution to the exchequer. They were abolished by Robert Peel's government in 1846.

Pitt's Pictures and Daylight Robbery
A window into revenue-generation

Window tax was first introduced in 1696. Each dwelling with any windows had to pay a tax of two shillings (10p); those with ten to twenty windows paid four shillings; those with more than twenty windows paid eight shillings. Certain poor families were exempted and the tax may be compared with the later rates and council tax. It was easy to assess but,

like all taxes, it was unpopular and regarded by some as 'a tax on light and air'. It may also be the origin of the expression 'daylight robbery' and some householders managed to reduce their payments by bricking up their windows, a feature of some of the buildings in the fashionable financial district of Charlotte Square in Edinburgh. These became known as 'Pitt's Pictures' when the Window Tax was increased by William Pitt the Younger in the 1780s. Some wealthy families, however, decided that the construction of houses with many windows was a way of drawing attention to their affluence. By 1815 the tax was raising the very substantial sum of £2 million a year to pay for the Napoleonic Wars. The tax was finally abolished in 1851, coincidentally the year of the Great Exhibition staged in Joseph Paxton's Crystal Palace, an incredible erection of cast iron and acres of glass which was

followed by the construction of many similar buildings.

William Pitt Strikes Again
Income tax: just a temporary arrangement, right?

Income tax had long been resisted on the grounds that the disclosure of income that it required was a gross intrusion on personal liberty (besides the less noble reason that people just didn't want to pay it). It was introduced as a 'temporary' measure in 1799 by William Pitt the Younger to finance the wars against France and in 1816, as the wars ended, the tax was abolished. However the gradual

The Thames Embankment

expansion of government activities in the 19th century into fields like education, sanitation, the Poor Law and local government required its 'temporary' reintroduction in 1842. Thereafter numerous governments, including those of both Gladstone and Benjamin Disraeli (1804–1881), tried to abolish it again but without success. As late as the 1870s Gladstone tried to lay his hands on some land which had been reclaimed from the Thames by the Metropolitan Board of Works. The Board used the land to create the Victoria Embankment but Gladstone tried to claim some surplus plots to build offices whose rents, he hoped, would generate enough revenue to do away with income tax. A petition to the Queen organized by the MP and newspaper seller W H Smith frustrated this noble plan so, as well as income tax, we now also have Victoria Embankment Gardens free of Gladstone's proposed offices. The highest rate of income tax was reached in World War II when surtax, on incomes above £2,000, amounted to nineteen shillings and sixpence (97.5p) in the pound!

MINIMUM WAGE FIXED AT THE LOCAL PUB

After the general election of 1997 the Labour government instituted the minimum wage, but it wasn't the first time this had been done in British history. In 1795 the magistrates of Speenhamland (now Speen) on the outskirts of Newbury in Berkshire, met at an inn called The Pelican to discuss the distress caused by high grain prices which were the result of a poor harvest. They decreed that the wages of the industrious poor would be topped up from the rates in relation to the price of a gallon loaf. The gallon loaf weighed almost

9 pounds and since this cost one shilling (5p) then a working man was guaranteed a weekly wage of three shillings for himself and his wife and a further one shilling and sixpence (7.5p) for each child. This humane measure did nothing to encourage farmers and other employers to pay their workforces a living wage since they knew that the wages would be topped up from the rates. Nevertheless the system was widely adopted, especially in the south of England, and became a severe burden on the rates. It survived until the Poor Law Amendment Act of 1834, advocated by Edwin Chadwick, which decreed that those unable to support themselves would be sent to workhouses where the conditions would be no more 'eligible' (i.e. humane) than necessary to keep the residents alive. In these circumstances only those truly desperate would enter those dreaded establishments. The workhouse system was abolished in 1930 but many of the buildings remained in use as offices and hospitals. The concept of the minimum wage had to wait until 1997 to be reintroduced.

Swamps and Midges Spread Diseases
Scotland declared bankrupt chasing an American dream

In 1696 the 'Company of Scotland' appealed to the citizens of Edinburgh for the huge sum of £400,000 to finance its plans to exploit the untold riches of the Darien isthmus of Panama with its gold deposits and limitless forests of valuable timber. They had been encouraged in this by an English ship's surgeon called Lionel Wafer who had returned from the area and supposedly seen these treasures. Wafer's cause had been taken up by William Paterson, a Scotsman who had helped to form the Bank of England two years earlier. Paterson first tried to interest London financiers who were sceptical of Wafer's claims. The 'Company of Scotland' was more successful. In the words of one director the Scottish investors 'came in shoals from every corner of the kingdom, rich, poor, blind, lame, to lodge their subscriptions in the company's house'. In a few days most of Scotland's savings were invested in the scheme. In 1698 the fleet of six ships set out, laden with serge cloth, wigs, shoes and 380 Bibles to trade with the Cuna Indians who inhabited the Darien isthmus.

Precious little gold: Darien scheme collapses

Upon arrival it very quickly became apparent that the area, while well supplied with poisonous snakes and biting insects, had little useable timber and no gold. Moreover the Cuna Indians, though friendly, had no interest in serge cloth in the tropical heat. The most telling indication of the hopelessness of the venture lies in the reaction of the Spanish authorities who governed the lands on either side of Panama.

They had omitted to colonize the area themselves because they knew it to be an inhospitable, disease-ridden swamp. In 1534 the Spaniards had considered the possibility of cutting a canal through Panama but abandoned it as a hopeless venture and even in the 20th century the eventual cutting of the canal cost almost 30,000 lives. The Spaniards were content to leave the intruding Scots alone to die of tropical diseases. The colonists, however, were undeterred. They wrote to their compatriots back in Edinburgh that 'the wealth, fruitfulness, health and good situation of the country proves much above our greatest expectation', naming the colony New Caledonia and the first settlement New Edinburgh. Moreover, in an attempt to raise more

capital and recruit more colonists, they produced maps which showed such features as 'Place where, upon digging for stones to make an oven, a considerable mixture of gold was found in them'. The second fleet of colonists was no more fortunate than the first and in the meantime the Spaniards, under orders from Madrid, had stirred themselves to take action against the by-now thoroughly demoralized intruders. In March 1700 the Scots agreed to evacuate the colony. The Spaniards took pity on the survivors and obligingly towed their ships out to sea. Most of them died on the return to Scotland from sickness or shipwreck. The Darien scheme effectively wrecked the finances of Scotland and was widely derided in the English press. The virtual bankruptcy of the nation helped to drive the Scots into the Act of Union with England which marked the end of the Scottish Parliament for almost 300 years. The English government paid the Scots £400,000 to restore the financial health of the nation, some of which went to the shareholders of the 'Company of Scotland'. It was poor

compensation for what was, in effect, the loss of financial and political independence. One person who emerged unscathed from the scheme was Lionel Wafer, who started it all. The Scots had promised him a share in the scheme in return for his information about the gold and timber of Darien but they reneged on the agreement and excluded him from it as an untrustworthy 'Sassenach'. A piece of luck for him!

THE BAGPIPES: APPROPRIATED BY THE SCOTS

Perhaps it was to console themselves for the loss of their Parliament that the Scots appropriated the bagpipes in the 18th century. The Emperor Nero is recorded (not in audio format, sadly) as playing an instrument with his mouth and armpit in the 1st century AD and the instrument is mentioned, by name, in Chaucer's **Canterbury Tales** *in about 1380. In the 16th century the instrument was associated chiefly with Ireland and is today played in many places including Serbia, Poland and Brittany. But in the 18th century*

the Scots made the instrument their own, particularly in connection with Highland regiments which carried the instrument to every corner of the British Empire. In Scotland it is associated with New Year's Eve celebrations ('Hogmanay'), with piping in the haggis on Burns Night and, heroically, with the late Glaswegian Piper Bill Millin who piped ashore the British commandos in the thick of the Normandy beach fighting on D-Day. Piping on the orders of Lord Lovat and contrary to the specific instructions of General Montgomery, Bill Millin survived that ordeal (the Germans didn't shoot at him because they thought he was mad) and died in August 2010.

The South Sea Bubble Bursts

Prototype financial crisis caused by investments no-one understood

Britain in 1720 was a place of great optimism. The War of the Spanish Succession had ended with a series of resounding victories by the Duke of Marlborough's armies over those of Louis XIV. The Treaty of Utrecht, which marked the end of the conflict in 1713, granted Britain the right to send one ship a year to trade with Mexico, Peru or Chile. On this very flimsy basis the South Sea Company was authorized to raise the huge sum of £2 million, with the promise of riches beyond the dreams of avarice from the El Dorado which many believed to lie in South America.

The value of the company's stock soared, on one occasion trebling in value in a single day. One of the few who were sceptical amidst the general euphoria was the Prime Minister, Robert Walpole (1676–1745), whose views on the subject were so unpopular that the chamber of the House of Commons emptied when he rose to speak on the matter, as MPs who had invested in the venture fled from his warnings. Other similar ventures quickly followed. They included a company devoted to creating a perpetual motion machine, one for manufacturing square cannon balls to be used against infidels and another 'for carrying on an undertaking of great advantage but nobody to know what it is'. In August the value of the company's stock was changing hands for ten times the price at its launch in February but the company still hadn't done any business and rumours began to circulate that the directors who had launched the company had sold out and cashed in their profits, as indeed they had. The value of the company collapsed, the treasurer, Mr Knight, fled to France and the Chancellor of the Exchequer, who had supported the company in Parliament, was sent to the Tower of London and burned in effigy. Only Walpole had his reputation strengthened. This was the first major financial fiasco in London – but by no means the last.

LOUIS XIV BOOSTS BRITISH ECONOMY

Walpole's government was inadvertently helped with its finances by the French king Louis XIV (reigned 1643–1715). In 1685 Louis XIV revoked the Edict of Nantes which, since 1598, had granted freedom of worship to French Protestants, known as Huguenots. The origin of the word 'Huguenot' is a mystery but there was nothing mysterious about the fate of this enterprising and patriotic group of French citizens once the persecutions began after 1685. They were, in effect, unprotected by French law and in the months that followed the revocation

more than 200,000 of France's citizens emigrated to more tolerant countries, notably to the Netherlands and Britain – both of which would be ruled by the Protestant William of Orange. At the Battle of the Boyne in 1690, which ensured his triumph over the deposed and exiled Catholic king James II, William was served by over 1,000 French Huguenot soldiers, many of whom served later in the campaigns of the Duke of Marlborough. Marlborough's armies destroyed those of France during the War of the Spanish Succession which clouded the last years of Louis' reign. Huguenots also brought many industrial skills with them which benefited the British economy. The silk-weaving industry of Spitalfields in London and the lace-making of Nottingham can trace their origins to Huguenot refugees. Many famous British men and women are also descended from Huguenot ancestors, amongst them the actors David Garrick and Laurence Olivier, the writer Daphne du Maurier, the industrialist and art patron Samuel Courtauld, the comedian Eddie Izzard, the Rolling Stone

Keith Richards, Francis Beaufort who devised the Beaufort Scale for measuring wind speed and Winston Churchill. What would Louis XIV have thought of the consequences of his intolerance?

That's Got to Hurt
Punishments of the Infamous, Pecuniary and Corporal varieties

In 1582 William Lambard of Lincoln's Inn applauded the fact that the English penal code no longer included 'pulling out the tongue for false rumours, cutting off the nose for adultery, taking away the privy parts for counterfeiting money' or certain other medieval penalties. Even so, the remaining punishments, which Lambard divided into three groups, included

The Ducking-Stool

some formidable deterrents to misbehaviour:

Infamous punishments, for such crimes as treason: notably being hung, drawn and quartered.

Pecuniary punishments for swearing, failing to attend church or playing a musical instrument on the Sabbath, etc: mostly fines imposed by Justices of the Peace which, rather like parking fines, helped to pay for the local system of government and justice.

Corporal punishments, divided into two categories: 'Capital (or deadly) punishment is done sundry ways as by hanging, burning, boiling or pressing'; 'Not Capital is of diverse forms as of cutting off the hand or ear, burning, whipping, imprisoning, stocking, setting in the pillory or ducking stool.'

CAN'T TOUCH THIS
Malefactors could avoid all these penalties by seeking sanctuary in the church of St Martin's le Grand in the City of London which dated from 1056 and possibly earlier. Although the foundation was dissolved by Henry VIII it retained rights of sanctuary until 1697. One who sought refuge there was Miles Forrest,

one of those held responsible for the murder of the Princes in the Tower. In 1829 it became the site of the headquarters of the Post Office. It is close to the former site of Newgate, now the Old Bailey.

'Pressing' was a particularly unpleasant ordeal reserved for those who refused to enter a plea. If a person was found guilty of a crime his possessions were confiscated by the Crown, leaving his family destitute. If no plea was entered his estate remained with the family. Weights, usually heavy stones, would be placed upon his prostrate body until he relented or died or both. This was known as *Peine Forte et Dure* (strong and hard penalty) and was last used at Cambridge Assizes in 1741 though not abolished until 1772. For women, the alternative was to suffer cords being tied tightly around the thumbs, as inflicted upon Mary Andrews in 1721 until her thumbs snapped.

THE CATO STREET CONSPIRACY
The last people to be sentenced to be hung, drawn and quartered were

the Cato Street Conspirators who planned to murder the Cabinet while they were at dinner in 1820. Their plan was to parade the heads of their victims, impaled on poles, thereby inciting a revolution after which the land of Great Britain would be equally divided amongst the population. The leader was Arthur Thistlewood but the plot was thoroughly infiltrated and when the plotters arrived at their rendezvous in Cato Street, Marylebone (now marked by a plaque) they were arrested by twelve 'Bow Street Runners'. Five were sentenced to transportation and five, including Thistlewood, to be hung, drawn and

quartered. However the hangman ensured they were all dead before cutting them down and beheading them. He then lifted up each and, in accordance with tradition, cried 'Behold the head of a traitor'. As the last head slipped from his grasp onto the execution platform the crowd cried 'Butterfingers!'

Anything but Prison
Incarceration or the army

Imprisonment as a penalty was unusual until well into the 19th century. Prisons were expensive to run and were mostly used to detain people before their trials or, if condemned to death, to hold them for the few days before they were executed. Begging was looked upon particularly severely. 'Idle and disorderly persons' and 'rogues and vagabonds' were to be publicly whipped before being returned to the parishes of their birth. 'Incorrigible rogues' were to be offered to the Army, these penalties being imposed by Justices of the Peace (JP).

I FOUGHT THE LAW – AND THE LAW WON

The ancient office of Justice of the Peace is first mentioned in a statute of 1361 but it is clear from the context that the statute is referring to an institution that had already existed for some time, probably from the reign of Richard I when we read of Keepers of the Peace. The local Justices, also known as magistrates, were responsible for administering justice for most offences and for rounding up serious offenders to await the arrival of the king's judges who could impose more severe penalties in Assize Courts. JPs were also responsible, outside the chartered boroughs, for the administration of local government in such matters as repairing roads and bridges. There are at present about 30,000 JPs in England and Wales who continue to dispose of about 96 per cent of criminal cases, the remaining 4 per cent being sent by them to the Crown Courts which replaced the Assize Courts in 1972. The work is voluntary and unpaid, as it has always been.

The Bloody Code
The unexpected risks to impersonating a pensioner

From 1688 the number of crimes punishable by death gradually increased until by 1830 about 300 offences were in this category. They included stealing something worth more than five shillings (25p) which even in 1830 was only a day's wages; impersonating a Chelsea Pensioner; the poaching of deer; and damaging Westminster Bridge. Many judges and juries, recognising the absurdity of the system, either refused to convict or declared that goods stolen

were worth less than five shillings. Commentators such as the Anglican clergyman William Paley argued that the hanging of thieves was correct because 'property, being more exposed, requires the terror of capital punishment to protect it'. He further argued that, although the prospect of hanging should be available for many crimes, it should rarely be inflicted, leaving the deterrent in place but without its excessive use!

THE YORKSHIRE GUILLOTINE

This infamous device was invented to ensure a swift death by beheading and to avoid the consequences of inefficient (or occasionally drunken) executioners missing their mark. Its invention is usually attributed to the French Dr Joseph-Ignace Guillotin (1738–1814) and its use is associated with the executions which followed the French Revolution in 1789. However it had many predecessors. The Halifax Gibbet is recorded in the Yorkshire town in the late 13th century, the blade being an axe head attached to a wooden block which slid up and down in fifteen foot-high uprights surmounted by a horizontal beam. It remained in use until 1650. A similar device is shown in a picture called 'The execution of Murdoch Ballagh near to Merton in Ireland, 1307'.

EXTRAORDINARY BRITONS

Britain has produced an amazing number of extraordinary people, not all of them pleasant individuals. Some of them deserve to be better-known.

The Great Outlaw
The many faces of Robin Hood

In the grounds of Kirklees Priory near Mirfield in Yorkshire is a grave which bears the name Robin Hood. Across the border in Derbyshire in St Michael's churchyard, Hathersage, is the grave of Little John from which, in 1780, a thigh bone was removed which would have belonged to a man about 8 feet tall. 'Robin Hood's' grave is empty but the gravestone has been moved more than once and bits of an earlier one were chewed as a supposed remedy for toothache! A medieval document records that in 1225 a fugitive called Robert Hood had goods confiscated to the value of 32 shillings and sixpence (£1.62.5p) for failing to appear in a Yorkshire court. In 1262 a similar forfeit was paid by a fugitive called Robehod in

Berkshire, again for non-appearance in court. The legends of Robin Hood gathered pace in the 15th century. The best researched – that of the Scotsman John Mair, written in 1521 – claimed that Robin Hood was outlawed in 1193, the time with which the legends traditionally associate him. The early accounts recorded the presence of Little John with Robin Hood, operating in Yorkshire, Nottinghamshire and Derbyshire and coming into conflict with a Eustace of Lowdham who was, in reality, at various times sheriff of Yorkshire and Nottinghamshire. Robin Hood plays emerged, usually performed in the springtime, at which the Robin Hood character collected money from wealthy churchgoers for the benefit of the poor. The most authentic of all the Robin Hood characters was a renegade clergyman called Robert Stafford of Lindfield, near Haywards Heath in Sussex. Between 1417 and 1429 he led a band of robbers and, at some point, started to call himself Friar Tuck. Maid Marion first appeared in a French play of 1283 and, like Friar Tuck, became attached to the Robin Hood legend, perhaps to give what Hollywood would later call 'love interest'. Despite the persistent Nottingham connection Robin Hood has been annexed by Yorkshire tourist and transport board which has named an airport after him just outside Doncaster.

Will the Schoolmaster?
Shakespeare's lost years

Little is known for sure about William Shakespeare's life as a young man. He was born in 1564, married Anne Hathaway in 1582, saw the birth of a daughter, Susanna, six months after the marriage and of twins, Judith and Hamnet, in 1585. In about 1616, the year of Shakespeare's death, a clergyman called Richard Davies claimed that Shakespeare, as a young man, had poached rabbits and deer from the Charlecote estate of Sir Thomas Lucy who had Shakespeare whipped and gaoled, prompting him to leave Stratford. Charlecote did have a rabbit warren on which deer could well have been grazing. This contemporary account was picked up by a later tradition which held that Shakespeare took his revenge by portraying Lucy as Justice Shallow in *The Merry Wives of Windsor* and lampooned Lucy's coat of arms by

referring to louses (lucys). Later in the 17th century John Aubrey, in his Brief Lives, quoted the son of one of Shakespeare's fellow actors, Christopher Beeston, as claiming that Shakespeare had been a 'schoolmaster in the country'. Beeston would have had no reason to lie about this. This account is supported by a persistent tradition which links Shakespeare with the Lancashire-based Hoghton family at their home near Preston, the connection with the family being a schoolmaster called John Cottom who taught in Stratford during Shakespeare's schooldays and whose family home was near that of the Hoghtons. A Hoghton will of the time mentions 'William Shakeshaft now dwelling with me'. The Hoghtons were Catholics and a document of 1592 records Shakespeare's father as a recusant (refusing to take Anglican communion) while another of 1606 lists the poet's daughter, Susanna, in the same vein. Some scholars have detected Catholic sympathies in Shakespeare's plays (but then Hitler found things in Shakespeare's works that he liked so perhaps that doesn't

mean too much). In 1608, while living in Stratford, Shakespeare took out a writ against John Addenbrooke for a debt. The name is unusual and a later John Addenbrooke (1681–1719) left money which founded the famous hospital which bears his name in Cambridge. This John Addenbrooke was descended from a family who lived in the West Midlands, not far from Shakespeare's home. So perhaps Shakespeare touched the family fortunes of this benefactor.

'A Certain Flush With Every Pull'
Inventing the lavatory

The WC was invented by Sir John Harington in 1596 but he only made two: one for himself and another for his godmother, Queen Elizabeth I. In 1778 Joseph Bramah (1748–1814), a Yorkshire carpenter and serial inventor, registered a patent which incorporated improvements to the design and made it possible to mass produce it from standard components. This he began to do in a workshop in Denmark Street,

close to the present site of Tottenham Court Road underground station. The device was quickly adopted by prosperous citizens and made Bramah's fortune. Its invention is sometimes wrongly attributed to Thomas Crapper. Crapper was a Victorian businessman who in 1861 opened a plumbing business in Chelsea. His only real contribution to the development of the WC was a memorable advertising slogan: 'a certain flush with every pull'! Joseph Bramah has many other inventions to his credit: a hydraulic press, a propelling pencil, a machine for numbering banknotes and a screw mechanism (as distinct from a paddle) for propelling ships. He also invented an 'unpickable lock' and offered a prize of £200 to anyone who could

overcome its ingenious mechanism. The prize was eventually claimed by an American called Alfred Hobbs who managed the feat over a period of 16 days at the Great Exhibition of 1851, 37 years after Bramah's death and 60 years after the challenge was issued.

SPENDING A PENNY

We owe this common expression to another Victorian businessman called George Jennings who in 1851 agreed to install his WCs in the Crystal Palace, home of the Great Exhibition in Hyde Park, provided that he could charge a penny per person. In this way the phrase 'spend a penny' entered the language as one of the more common euphemisms.

Curiosity Killed the Cat
Francis Bacon felled by frozen chicken

Francis Bacon (1561–1626) carried out one of the earliest experiments in food preservation. Bacon was a corrupt Lord Chancellor but is remembered as one of the fathers of modern science because of his insistence that theories should be tested by experiment. His last experiment occurred in 1626 when he stuffed a chicken carcass with snow in the belief that this would prevent it from decomposing. Unfortunately he did not find out, since he died shortly afterwards of pneumonia, probably contracted during the experiment. The lesson was not lost, however, since in 1663 Samuel Pepys recorded a conversation in a London coffee house: 'Fowl killed in December (Alderman Barker said) he did buy and, putting them into the box under

his sledge, did forget to take them out to eat 'til April next and were through the frost as sweet and fresh to eat as at first killed'. Clarence Birdseye did not come along with anything better until 1930.

Brain of Britain
The genius of Isaac Newton

Isaac Newton (1642–1727) was acknowledged by Albert Einstein as the greatest scientist who ever lived. His *Laws of Motion* are used to launch spacecraft and his exposition of the composition of white light still underpins the subject. His curiosity knew no limits. While he was developing his theory of colours he slipped a bodkin (a large needle) behind his eyeball to alter the curvature of the retina and discover its effect on the perception of colour. After this experiment he shut himself in the dark for several days to avoid the blindness that might have been expected. He later devoted much of his life to the study of the false science of Alchemy which attempted to turn base metals into gold and in support of this work developed a

German mathematician Gottfried Leibniz (1646–1716) who had had the temerity to devise the calculus at the same time as Newton himself. Newton set up a committee of the Royal Society to examine the rival claims, packed it with his friends and proceeded to write the committee's report himself. In 1696 Newton was appointed Warden of the Royal Mint with the task of reissuing the coinage which had been debased by 'clipping' by 'coiners' (snipping off bits of gold and silver and using the clippings to make more coins). He approached the task with his customary zeal and in less than three years produced twice as many new coins as had been produced in the previous thirty. He had himself made a magistrate, apprehended 28 'coiners' and had many of them hanged. In 1705 he became the first scientist to receive a knighthood. Many legends attached to his name are true. In 1697 the Swiss mathematician Johann Bernouilli set two problems to the mathematicians of Europe. Six months passed without a response. He then reissued the challenge. Newton returned to his rooms after a day at

theory that 'metalls vegetate'. He was not an easy man. At various points in his life he pursued feuds with his fellow scientist Robert Hooke (1635–1703) who felt that he had not received sufficient credit for information that had led Newton to formulate his Laws of Motion; and also with the Astronomer Royal John Flamsteed (1646–1719) who believed, with some reason, that Newton planned to take for himself much of the credit for the publication of Flamsteed's *Catalogue of Fixed Stars*. His greatest dispute was with the

the Mint, read the problem, wrote out the solutions and went to bed. The following day he posted the solutions to Bernouilli, omitting to sign the document. Bernouilli stated that he recognized Newton's hand 'as the lion is recognized by its paw'. The story of the apple falling from the tree was told by Newton himself in his lifetime and passed by Newton's niece to the French writer Voltaire who, on observing the elaborate funeral for Newton in Westminster Abbey, commented that 'the English honour a mathematician as other nations honour a king'. When he died Alexander Pope composed an appropriate epitaph:

Nature and Nature's Laws lay hid in night,
God said 'Let Newton be' and all was light

Doctor Pox
Edward Jenner's gamble

Until the 19th century, smallpox was widespread, often lethal and left its surviving victims (including Queen Elizabeth I) disfigured by scars. Edward Jenner (1749–1823) was

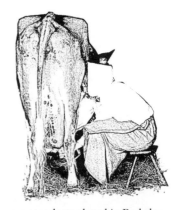

a country doctor based in Berkeley, Gloucestershire. Milkmaids had a reputation for beauty and Jenner noted that, while they frequently carried blisters on their hands, known as cowpox, from handling the udders of cows, they never developed the pustules of smallpox. He concluded that cowpox protected them so he extracted some pus from the blisters of a milkmaid called Sarah Nelmes and injected it into James Phipps, the eight-year-old son of his gardener. James remained well so Jenner then deliberately injected James with smallpox, a potentially deadly disease. Nowadays this would lead to his being struck off the medical register. Fortunately for James and for the reputation of Jenner, the boy remained free of smallpox. The practice of vaccination spread rapidly, though not without opposition. Dr Benjamin Mosley (1742–1819) described the practice as 'the ravings of Bedlam' and another condemnation came from a surprising quarter: Alfred Russell Wallace (1823–1919) who, with Charles Darwin, developed the theory of evolution. But others, including Napoleon and a delegation of Native American chiefs praised and rewarded him. Edward Jenner was also a keen naturalist and was the first to observe the habit of the young cuckoo in expelling other eggs from the nest which it occupied.

All Steamed Up
Who really invented the steam engine?

The invention of the steam engine is often attributed to James Watt or George Stephenson but in reality they simply improved on the designs of others, all of them being British. The first patent for 'a new invention for raising water by the important use of fire' was registered by Thomas

Savery (c.1650–1715). His machine was designed to pump water out of tin mines. Steam was introduced under pressure into a sealed vessel, driving a piston to force water up a pipe and out of the mine. Cold water was then sprinkled on the vessel to condense the steam so that the piston fell back. Savery later went into partnership with Thomas Newcomen (1663–1729), a Devon blacksmith, who introduced a piston attached to a beam so that the pressure could be applied to the water as the piston fell as well as when it rose under pressure, thereby doubling its effectiveness. However the process of heating and cooling was extravagant in the use of energy. The contribution of James

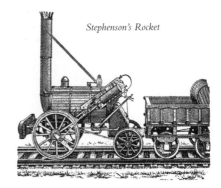

Stephenson's Rocket

Watt (1736–1819) was to use a valve to release the steam from the piston cylinder into a separate condenser so that the process of continuously heating and cooling the mechanism was no longer needed.

THE KETTLE LID

The tale that James Watt was influenced by seeing the lid of a kettle rise as it boiled was long thought to be a myth. However a letter written by Watt and auctioned in London in March 2003 specifically mentions the incident.

These engines were heavy and needed large stocks of water and coal to power them. They were therefore only suitable as stationary engines in factories (or ships) and it took Richard Trevithick (1771–1833), 'the Cornish Giant', to devise a steam engine which would move on land. This he did by putting the heating source, a metal tube, inside the boiler so that all the heat generated by the fire was transferred to the water, none being lost to the surrounding atmosphere. His steam locomotive successfully climbed a hill outside Camborne in Cornwall on Christmas Eve, 1801, but Trevithick's ingenuity was not accompanied by financial acumen and he died destitute.

Stephenson's Rocket

Finally George (1781–1848) and Robert (1803–1859) Stephenson made further improvements by putting multiple tubes into the boiler, thereby increasing the amount of heat transferred and by placing the piston at a 45 degree angle to the wheel, thereby imparting motion more efficiently. So it took a lot of people to design Stephenson's Rocket.

STEPHENSON AND THE ELECTRIC TRAIN

On 4th April 1912 **The Times** *published a letter from a correspondent who had worked for a Newcastle firm part-owned by George Stephenson. In 1847, the year before his death, Stephenson had visited the firm and said 'I have the credit of being the inventor of the locomotive and it is true I have done something to improve the action of steam for that purpose. But I tell you, young man, I shall not live to see it but you may, a time when electricity will be the great motive power of the world.'*

Half Nelsons
Horatio the family man

When Nelson died at Trafalgar a grateful nation conferred a substantial pension of £2,000 a year on his wife Frances, from whom he had been estranged for six years. He had married Frances, an attractive and charming widow, while serving in the West Indies.

The future William IV was best man at the wedding. The marriage was childless but Frances was a faithful and loving wife, supporting Nelson from 1788–93 while he languished, unemployed and on half pay, at the family home in Norfolk. On Nelson's death a peerage was conferred on his brother William which remains in the family. The 9th Earl Nelson, better known as detective sergeant Peter Nelson of Hertfordshire police service, died in March 2009 and was succeeded by his son Simon, also a policeman. Nelson did, however, have an illegitimate daughter, Horatia, by his mistress Emma Hamilton for whom he deserted Frances. Horatia was baptized Horatia Thompson in 1801 to disguise her paternity and then 'adopted' by Nelson and Emma. Horatia cared for the alcoholic Emma at Emma's last home in Calais where she died in 1815 and Horatia later married Philip Ward, a curate to Nelson's clergyman father, by whom she had ten children. Horatia herself survived to 1881 and is buried at Pinner, in Middlesex. Nelson's closest living descendant is Anna Horatia Tribe, his great-great-great grand-daughter who lives in Raglan, Monmouthshire.

'Such a Damned Fool'
The Iron Duke's affairs

Arthur Wellesley (1769–1852), descendant of an Anglo-Irish family, was not a promising child. Awkward and dull at Eton he was thought fit only for a military career, a common choice for stolid sons of the aristocracy, and sent to the Academy of Equitation at Angers in 1786 – so he received his military training from his future enemy, the French! From 1787–92 he held commissions in six separate regiments without working in any of them since he was serving as a Member of the Irish Parliament for the family borough of Trim in County Meath. In 1793 he proposed to Catherine Pakenham, but was rejected because he would not be able to support her. He went to serve with the army in India, earned a reputation as a commander and a significant income and returned to England in 1805 when he had his only meeting with Nelson, a month before Trafalgar. He was not impressed, at first finding the notoriously egotistical admiral 'vain and silly'. In 1806 he wrote to Catherine, whom he had not seen for twelve years, again proposing marriage. This time he was accepted but regretted his proposal upon meeting her, declaring 'She has grown ugly, by Jove'. The marriage produced two sons but was unhappy. He found the short-sighted and nervous 'Kitty' irritating and clinging and in 1822 asked a female confidante, Harriet Arbuthnot 'Would you have believed that anyone could have been such a damned fool? I was not the least in love with her. I married her because they asked me to do it'. His liaison with the courtesan Harriette Wilson elicited his famous observation 'Publish and be damned'.

HARRIETTE WILSON: DAMNED

Harriette Dubouchet was the daughter of a clockmaker who, along with her two sisters and her niece, adopted the career of courtesan becoming the mistress of many leading citizens including the Prince Regent, the future George IV. She was later known as Harriette Wilson or Mrs Q and in 1825 announced that **she would be publishing Memoirs of Harriette Wilson,** *Written by Herself. The announcement was accompanied by the declaration that a payment of £200 would ensure that the payer would not be mentioned in the book. It was this offer that provoked the Duke's response 'Publish and be damned'. The publisher's offices were besieged by eager buyers and the book ran to 30 editions in its first year. It earned £10,000 for its author, plus any 'fees' paid by those of her amours who were less resilient than the Iron Duke. Sir Walter Scott commented that 'The gay world has been kept in hot water lately by this impudent publication'.*

When Kitty died in 1831 Wellington showed her memory some belated affection but his closest female friend was Harriet Arbuthnot. She was his friend but not his lover and when she died she was mourned equally by Wellington and her husband Charles, a Tory minister. Charles then moved to Wellington's home, Apsley House, and lived there until his death in 1850.

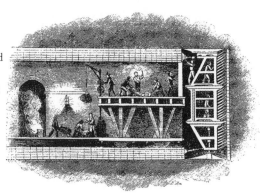

Brunel's tunnelling shield

Chip Off the Old Block
Brunel's less famous father

Most people know of Isambard Kingdom Brunel (1806–1859), engineer of the Great Western Railway, but few know of his equally ingenious father Sir Marc Brunel (1769–1849) who invented the Tunnelling Shield. It was a cast iron frame which was placed up against the area to be excavated, thereby protecting from falling debris the labourers who worked within it, excavating the surface ahead of them. It was used to create the world's first tunnel beneath a river, the Thames Tunnel, between Wapping and Rotherhithe. It took 18 years to build (1825–43) and was dogged by problems. These included floods which drowned several workers and nearly killed Isambard; and bankruptcy from which it was rescued by a government loan. Originally dubbed The Eighth Wonder of the World it lost sackfuls of money. It was sold in 1865 to the East London Railway so that oft-forgotten corner of the underground railway system has the distinction of being carried beneath the Thames by the world's oldest tunnel under a river. Tunnelling shields based on Marc Brunel's design have been used for cutting the London tube railways, the Channel Tunnel and virtually every other tunnel of any size since.

The Reluctant Clergyman
Charles Darwin's early years

In the autumn of 1828 Charles Darwin (1809–1882) arrived at Christ's College, Cambridge. It was not a promising start. He had already attended Edinburgh University to study medicine but left because he could not bear to watch operations being carried out in the era before anaesthetics. He arrived in Cambridge three weeks late, was consequently put into rooms above a nearby shop (now Boots the chemist) and unpacked his new £20 shotgun and beetle collection before setting off on a round of card-playing, drinking, hunting and gambling. The plan was for him to become a clergyman but his father and tutors despaired of him. His father wrote that he would be good for nothing but rat-catching and, having witnessed

with approval a student riot, Darwin acknowledged that he could have been sent down from the university. Instead of studying theology he devoted his energy to collecting insects and attending lectures on botany and geology. The professor of botany, John Henslow, must have seen some promise in him because when Henslow was offered the post of naturalist on board HMS *Beagle* during its five-year journey round the world, he turned down the opportunity and recommended Charles Darwin instead. The result was *On the Origin of Species*, perhaps the most controversial book ever published, since it overturned all that Victorians, especially clergymen, believed about the creation of the world. But the strength of his arguments was irresistible and he was soon forgiven. In 1877 Cambridge awarded him an honorary doctorate and in 1882 he was buried in Westminster Abbey.

Immortalized in Print
Dickens's dysfunctional family

Charles Dickens's eminence as a writer is assured but his novels often reflect experiences, especially in childhood, with which he could never come to terms. Those who loved him sometimes bore the consequences. His father John was a genial and improvident man whose bankruptcy and brief sojourn in a debtors' prison was a source of shame that Dickens only ever mentioned to two people: his wife Catherine and one close friend. His father was a model for one of his most memorable characters. Mr Micawber in *David Copperfield*, a genial and impecunious optimist

Mr Micawber

whom it is impossible to dislike, is certainly based on John Dickens and reflects the son's affection for, and exasperation with, his father. A family connection enabled Dickens to obtain a poorly paid job as a journalist and his talent soon earned him promotion to better paid work but it was in his early, straitened years that he fell in love with Maria Beadnell, the daughter of a wealthy banker and failed to win her because of his lowly status. In 1836 success came with his first major work, *The Pickwick Papers*. By this time he had lost Maria Beadnell to another man and he married Catherine Hogarth, possibly because of a physical resemblance to Maria. The marriage was not a happy one though it produced eight surviving children. By 1855 Dickens was writing that 'the skeleton in my domestic closet is becoming a pretty big one'. He leaked false information to the effect that Catherine was a poor mother and mentally unstable and boarded up the door between their bedrooms. Catherine was portrayed in *David Copperfield* as the simple-minded Dora Spenlow. In the meantime he had met Maria Beadnell again after an interval of 10 years and, finding her married and unattractive, made her the subject of an unflattering portrait as Flora Finching in *Little Dorrit*. In 1857, aged 45, he fell in love with a 17-year-old actress called Ellen ('Nelly') Ternan. He despatched Catherine to a separate home and wrote a short story about a man who willed to death a wife whose cloying devotion he found intolerable. His relationship with Nelly was probably not consummated and was carefully concealed in his lifetime – though he had a narrow escape, in two respects, when he was travelling with Nelly in a train which crashed at Staplehurst in Kent in 1865. Ten people died, Dickens was uninjured and Nelly was spirited away from the scene. The relationship did not become known until 1934. Dickens died in 1870, still loved by Catherine. When she died in 1879 she asked her daughter to bequeath his early love letters to the British Museum 'that the world may know he loved me once'.

The Lady with the Calculator
Florence Nightingale's gift for maths

The life of Florence Nightingale (1820–1910) as a nurse is well known. Less celebrated are her achievements as a mathematician, though these underpinned her work in public health campaigns. Karl Pearson (1857–1936), a professor at University College, London, declared, 'Were I a man of wealth I would see that Florence Nightingale was commemorated not only as the "Lady

of the Lamp" but by the activities of the "Passionate Statistician",' and Florence herself wrote that statistics were 'the cipher by which we may read the thoughts of God'. Her precocious interest in the subject dismayed her father who considered the subject unfeminine. She was largely self-taught and used her grasp of statistics to draw attention to the connection between poor housing, poor sanitation and disease. She was frustrated by the ignorance of mathematics amongst public figures, and in 1891 she wrote that 'though the great majority of Cabinet Ministers, of the Army, of the Executive, of both Houses of Parliament, have received a University Education, what has that University Education taught them of the practical application of statistics?' In despair at the innumeracy which she encountered she devised a 'coxcomb' diagram 'to affect through the Eyes what we may fail to convey through their word-proof ears'. It was an early and sophisticated pie chart. Her greatest allies in her campaigns were Queen Victoria and Prince Albert. After lengthy interviews with the royal couple at Balmoral,

the queen wrote, 'We have made Miss Nightingale's acquaintance and are delighted and very much struck by her great gentleness and simplicity and wonderfully clear and comprehensive head. I wish we had her at the War Office.' When Florence was dissatisfied with the reaction she received from politicians and officials to her reports, statistics, charts and diagrams she wrote to Victoria or Albert and received replies such as the one that greeted her analysis of the demographic consequences of the plan to move St Thomas's Hospital from London Bridge to its new home on the Albert Embankment. Prince Albert assured her that the matter 'has received the immediate attention any communication from you would be sure to command'. She was the first woman to be elected a Fellow of the (later Royal) Statistical Society, in 1858. In 1907 she was the first woman to be awarded the Order of Merit for her work in improving the health of the nation but without her grasp of statistics she wouldn't have been able to identify so comprehensively the underlying causes of poor health.

The First Stamp
Rowland Hill's revolutionary idea

The Royal Mail dates from 1516 when Henry VIII appointed a Master of the Posts but it owes its fortune to Sir Rowland Hill (1795–1879) who in 1840, against much opposition to his 'wild and visionary scheme' introduced the penny post. His novel idea was that postage should be paid by the sender, in advance, thereby eliminating the need for postage to be collected at its destination, this being time-consuming and expensive. The result was the world's most famous postage stamp the Penny Black whose design, featuring the head of the young Queen Victoria, we owe to Sir Henry Cole (1808–1882). Since it was, at the time of its devising, the world's only adhesive postage stamp it was not considered necessary to identify the nation to which it belonged. The Royal Mail's stamps are still the only ones which do not bear the name of the nation that issues them. Henry Cole also devised the first commercial Christmas card and was the principal organizer of the Great Exhibition of 1851. The only remaining element to be devised was the pillar box – which was proposed by the novelist Anthony Trollope (1815–1882) who was in charge of the eastern postal district of England from 1859–66, and who realized that in rural areas there was much inconvenience involved in taking letters to a post office in a town.

Unforeseen Consequences
Alexander Graham Bell's aid for the deaf

Alexander Graham Bell (1847–1922) was born in Edinburgh, the son of a professor who was an authority on speech disorders and a mother who suffered from growing deafness. His early interest centred on means by which speech could be made comprehensible to the deaf, and it was research into this which led to the invention of the telephone. In 1870 the family migrated to Canada and the young man attracted the patronage of a wealthy man called Gardiner Hubbard who hoped that Bell would be able to help his young daughter Mabel who had been rendered deaf by scarlet fever. Having familiarized himself with the technology of the early telegraphic systems which were beginning to cross America, in March 1876 Bell was awarded an American patent for 'the method of, and apparatus for, transmitting vocal or other sounds telegraphically'. In August of that year he made the first telephone call over a distance of two miles from Cambridge

to Boston, Massachusetts, and two years later he demonstrated the apparatus to Queen Victoria, making the first long distance telephone calls from her home at Osborne House on the Isle of Wight. The Queen's verdict: 'Most extraordinary'. A serial inventor, he later obtained 18 further patents in such diverse fields as alternative fuels and the phonograph (gramophone). He has the possibly unique distinction of being claimed by four nations, being numbered amongst the 10 greatest Scottish scientists; the 10 greatest Canadians; the 100 greatest Americans; and the 100 greatest Britons.

GREAT BRITISH ICON: THE RED TELEPHONE BOX

The first telephones in Britain were installed by the Post Office in Manchester in 1878 but the first public telephone kiosk had to wait until 1920. It was called K1 (Kiosk 1) and was a rather unattractive concrete structure of which one example survives, in Hull. London thought them too ugly for its streets so in 1924 the Royal Fine Art Commission instituted a competition which was won by the architect Giles

Gilbert Scott (1880–1960), who also designed Liverpool Cathedral and Battersea Power Station. He recommended that it be painted blue but red was chosen on the grounds that it would be more conspicuous, like pillar boxes for mail. This was almost its undoing since some areas outside London thought them out of keeping with their surroundings. Four further designs were developed from Scott's original one, the last of these being K6 – the Jubilee kiosk – to celebrate George V's silver jubilee in 1935. This was the first to be widely adopted outside the capital though some rural areas, thinking the red boxes too garish, painted them grey. The installation of telephones in homes, and later the widespread adoption of mobile phones, has meant the gradual phasing out of the familiar red boxes but as they have declined in number they have increased in popularity. Many have been bought as features for homes and gardens and their iconic status is reflected in the fact that many of those originally painted grey have now been repainted red.

A Formidable Sisterhood
The first lady doctor

Elizabeth Garrett Anderson (1836–1917) was the first woman to qualify as a female doctor in Britain. Prior to this, Margaret Ann Bulkley (c.1795–1865) had succeeded in working as a doctor in the army by living as a man named James Barry, though there is no consensus on this person's true status; and Elizabeth Blackwell (1821–1910) was born in Bristol but qualified as a doctor in New York before returning to Britain. Elizabeth Garrett Anderson, the daughter of an Aldeburgh corn

merchant, could not gain entry to a medical school but trained as a nurse at Middlesex Hospital and was allowed to attend lectures with male medical students until they asked for her to be removed because she proved much better than they were at answering questions. She learned that the Society of Apothecaries did not exclude women from their examinations which she duly sat and passed (at which point the Society changed its rules to prevent other women from following her). She obtained a medical degree in Paris (taking the examinations in French) and established a dispensary for women in London, which became the Elizabeth Garrett Anderson Hospital. In 1876 the General Medical Council finally agreed to admit women to the profession. In the 21st century the majority of students entering medical schools are young women. Elizabeth's sister, Millicent Garrett Fawcett, was a campaigner for women's causes, notably for the right to vote. The Fawcett Society is named in her memory.

No Lighthouse on Treasure Island
Robert Louis Stevenson's family trade

R obert Louis Stevenson (1850–1894) is best remembered as the author of one of the most enduring adventure stories, Treasure Island, but he should have been a civil engineer. His family were known as Lighthouse Stevensons because of their achievements in building lighthouses in some of the world's most dangerous seas. The author's grandfather, also called Robert Stevenson (1772–1850), was responsible for one of the most extraordinary achievements in civil

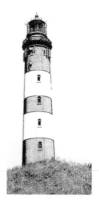

engineering when, in 1807–10, he built the Bell Rock Lighthouse, 12 miles off the east coast of Scotland, at a site where 70 ships had been wrecked in one storm alone. Such were the challenges of the task that in 2003 it was featured in a BBC series called *Seven Wonders of the Industrial World*. Built of Aberdeen granite, the structure has survived unscathed for over 200 years. The author's father and two uncles continued the family business and built lighthouses around the coasts of India, China, Japan, New Zealand and Singapore as well as Britain. Robert Louis Stevenson was spared entry into the family business because of his poor health which obliged him to live in warmer climes and enabled him to follow his chosen career of author. He died at his home at Vailima, Samoa, in the Pacific where he had sought refuge from the lung conditions that had plagued him from childhood, though the cause of his death was probably a cerebral haemorrhage.

Scouting for Boys and Girls
Baden-Powell mobilizes the young

The founder of the Scout movement was the son of a clergyman who died when he was three and a socially ambitious mother

who falsely claimed descent from Nelson, added the name Baden to the family name Powell and adopted, without reason, the coat of arms of the Dukes of Baden in Germany. Her son Robert Baden-Powell (1857–1941) failed the entrance examinations to both Balliol College and Christchurch Oxford (at a time when such examinations made few intellectual demands) and joined the army. He served initially with the Indian Army in Quetta (now

- 131 -

Pakistan) where he became an accomplished map maker and made his first contribution to literature with a volume called *Pig Sticking and Hog Hunting*, which told of his exploits in hunting wild boar. Faced with criticism that this was a cruel sport he wrote 'See how the horse enjoys it, see how the boar himself, mad with rage, rushes wholeheartedly into the scrap, see how you, with your temper thoroughly roused, enjoy the opportunity of wreaking it to the full. Yes, hog-hunting is a brutal sport – and yet I loved it.' He became a national figure during the Boer War when he organized the 219-day defence of Mafeking, a small town of little military value whose relief in May 1900 was the cause of national rejoicing. During the siege he used children to carry messages and this experience led to the formation of the Scout movement. In 1907 a camp for 22 boys including public schoolboys and the local Boys' Brigade (an innovation for the time) took place on Brownsea Island in Poole Harbour and was followed by *Scouting for Boys*, published in fortnightly instalments in 1908. By 1910 there were 100,000

scouts and in 1912, following an approach from some girls, Baden-Powell wrote *How Girls can Help Build up the Empire*. The Girl Guides were run by his formidable wife Olave, 32 years his junior, whom he married in the same year. There are at present almost 38 million scouts and guides in 216 countries. In 1929 he was made Baron Baden-Powell. Some of his ideas about the Empire now seem dated and he did have some idiosyncratic views on other matters. He recommended breathing through the nose, for example, thinking mouth breathing rather vulgar. But he founded what remains by far the largest youth movement in the world which received the double accolade of being banned by both Hitler and Stalin.

From Cavalry Charge to the Nuclear Deterrent
Churchill's epic career

Winston Churchill (1874–1965) has been voted the greatest ever Briton, though he was half-American through his mother, Jennie Jerome, who married his father, Randolph Churchill, the younger son of the Duke of Marlborough, in 1874. Churchill took part in the last cavalry charge of the British army at the battle of Omdurman in 1898 and ended his political career as Prime Minister in 1955 with authority over nuclear weapons. His career was by any standard an epic but before his 'finest hour' in 1940 he was often wrong or in the margins. In 1924, as Chancellor of the Exchequer, he returned Britain's currency to the gold standard at a rate of $4.86 to the pound which was too high for the economy to bear. It made British products (including coal) uncompetitive in the export market, helped lead to the General Strike of 1926 and made the collapse in the economy of the late 1920s worse than it needed to be. It was the memory of this phase of Churchill's career that helped to expel him from office in the election of 1945. In 1936 he attempted to rally support for King Edward VIII in his desire to marry Wallis Simpson and two days before the abdication he was shouted down in the House of Commons as he made a final, forlorn attempt to generate sympathy for the king's deservedly lost cause. And he resolutely opposed the granting of independence to India long after it had become inevitable, describing Mahatma Gandhi as 'a seditious middle temple lawyer, now posing as a fakir of a type well known in the east, striding half-naked up the steps of the viceregal palace'. But on the one thing that really mattered he was gloriously correct. When Hitler invaded Russia in June 1941 Churchill described him as a 'bloodthirsty guttersnipe' and, when questioned on his opposition to Communism, replied that 'If Hitler invaded Hell I would make at least a favourable reference to the Devil in the House of Commons'.

CHURCHILL AND THE WITCH

In the last year of the war Churchill became involved in the last 'witchcraft' trial in British history. Helen Duncan, a spiritualist, was alleged to have publicly revealed the sinking of the British battleship HMS **Barham** *before it was officially announced by the authorities. Contrary to Churchill's* *wishes she was prosecuted in 1944 under the 1735 Witchcraft Act for talking to spirits and spent 8 months in prison.*

Chapman of Tremadog?
aka Lawrence of Arabia

Thomas Edward Lawrence (1888–1935) was born in Tremadog, Caernarvonshire (now Gwynedd) in North Wales, one of five sons of Thomas Chapman and his mistress, Sarah Junner, for whom Chapman had deserted his wife. Sarah, who had been governess to the daughters of Chapman and his wife, was herself the illegitimate daughter of a man called Lawrence, and the couple adopted this name. The family was frequently on the move but eventually settled in Oxford. Sarah was profoundly religious and frequently at odds with young Thomas but in1908 a modus vivendi was reached when Thomas was given a bungalow at the bottom of the family garden where he could live apart from the family and indulge his interests which included medieval churches, castles and brass-rubbing. In 1907 he entered Jesus College Oxford and after graduating he worked from 1911–14 as an archaeologist in Syria. Here he acquired his knowledge of Arabic and his respect for the Arab peoples which, in 1916, led to his being assigned to the forces of Emir Faisal to lead the Arab revolt against the Turkish allies of the Germans in World War I. He was undoubtedly effective in harassing the Turkish troops by leading Arab forces to blow up railway lines and in capturing the port of Aqaba. The legend of 'Lawrence of Arabia' was promoted by an American journalist called Lowell Thomas in a slide show at Covent Garden after the war. At the war's end Lawrence attended the Versailles Conference, in Arab dress, as an adviser to Lloyd George, but failed to obtain a greater degree of independence for the Arab peoples. Lowell Thomas's version of his career was faithfully reproduced in David Lean's epic film of 1962. Lawrence's own works, notably *Revolt in the Desert*, did nothing to discourage the legend. Others have expressed some reservations. His famous scars appear to have been inflicted by beatings to which he subjected himself at the hands of young men from 1923, not at the hands of the Turks. After the war he was admitted to the RAF by Captain W E Johns (author of the *Biggles* stories) and worked on air-sea rescue seaplanes, one of the designers involved being R J Mitchell of Supermarine who went on to design the legendary Spitfire. In 1935 Lawrence died of head injuries following a motorcycle accident which led the doctor who examined him to recommend the universal adoption of crash helmets.

A controversial figure, he attracted the admiration and support of people as diverse as General Allenby, John Buchan and George Bernard Shaw.

On Her Majesty's Secret Service
Britain's famous spies

Britain's first spymaster was Sir Francis Walsingham (1532–1590) who ran Elizabeth I's secret service. His most notable triumph was to unmask the conspirators behind a plot to murder Elizabeth and replace her with Mary, Queen of Scots. Walsingham and his codebreakers knew that the most commonly used letter in the English language is 'e' so, having intercepted Mary's enciphered correspondence, they started by substituting 'e' for the most commonly used letter in the correspondence. They then worked through the alphabet using further common letters until they had enough to make sense of the messages. The penetration of the plot led directly to the execution of Mary in 1587 and that, in turn, to Philip of Spain's decision to launch the Spanish Armada a year later.

In October 1909 a naval officer, Commander Mansfield Cumming, and an army captain, Vernon Kell, occupied some premises at 64, Victoria Street, opposite the Army and Navy Stores in central London. The two men became, respectively, the heads of MI6 (the Secret Intelligence Service or SIS) and MI5, the domestic counter-intelligence Security Service. Cumming adopted the habit of writing in green ink and was referred to as 'C', both of these practices being followed by his successors, though in the James Bond films 007's boss is referred to as 'M' rather than 'C'. Cumming had a wooden leg and would alarm potential employees of MI6 in interviews by sticking a knife into it while they watched. Those who flinched were rejected by the service. He attempted to recruit the writer Compton McKenzie to the service, telling him that it was 'capital sport'. A worthy forebear of 007. In the early days spying was terribly gentlemanly. In September 1910 Lieutenant Siegfried Helm was arrested on suspicion of spying for his native Germany. Fortunately Helm

was both thorough and naïve and had kept a pocket book with sketches of Portsmouth's military defences, complete with details he had gleaned by looking through a large public 'penny-in-the-slot' telescope on Portsmouth seafront. Spying was then regarded as an act of patriotism and Helm wrote, while in prison awaiting trial, 'The officers here are very kind to me. So comfortable a time I never had'! The judge at his trial gave him a discharge and commented, 'I trust that when you leave this country you will leave it with a feeling that, although we may be vigilant yet we are just and merciful, not only to those who are subjects of this realm but also to those who, like yourself, seek the hospitality of these shores.'

Francis Walsingham was a graduate of King's College, Cambridge as was the most eminent of the Bletchley Park codebreakers, Alan Turing (1912–1954). The 'bombe' machine designed by Alan Turing was perhaps the most important invention of the war. At times it enabled German Enigma codes to be broken daily, within minutes, so that British commanders were sometimes reading Hitler's instructions to his generals before the Germans had decoded them. Bernard Montgomery sometimes claimed to be reading the mind of his German opponent Erwin Rommel. In fact he was reading his mail! It was long believed that the sinking of the formidable German battleship *Bismarck* was due to a chance sighting by a British aircraft, a belief reflected in the 1960 film *Sink the Bismarck*. This belief was held at a time when the existence of the codebreaking achievements of the Government Code & Cipher School (known as GCHQ today) at Bletchley Park were known only to a few. It was revealed much later that a German naval officer, knowing that the *Bismarck*, damaged, was being pursued, was concerned for the welfare of his son who was amongst the crew. He radioed to the ship to ask how far the ship was from port. The *Bismarck* replied reassuringly, giving her position, believing that the Enigma codes in which the message was sent were unbreakable. This told the Royal Navy where she was and led to her destruction. Alan Turing was persecuted

for his homosexuality and died in 1954 after taking a bite from an apple laced with cyanide. The symbol of Apple Computers is an apple with a bite-sized piece missing. Is this a tribute to Alan Turing, the father of modern computing, combined with a play on the word 'byte'? Steve Jobs, the co-founder of Apple, will neither confirm nor deny this suggestion.

Arthur Ransome – Superspy
Children's author or 'dangerous Bolshevik'?

Towards the end of World War I British politicians became concerned about a series of articles in the popular newspaper *Daily News* which were favourable to Lenin's Bolshevik regime in Russia. The author was Arthur Ransome. His pro-Bolshevik articles were a cover

The Bismarck

for the fact that he had infiltrated the inner circles of the Bolsheviks, befriending Leon Trotsky, the commissar for foreign affairs, with the aid of Trotsky's secretary, Evgenia Shelepina whom Ransome eventually married. There followed a game of cat and mouse in which Evgenia supplied Ransome with information about Bolshevik intentions while exposing herself to the risk of suspicion and the execution which would inevitably follow.

The Foreign Office denounced Ransome's 'dangerous Bolshevik' sympathies which so impressed the Bolsheviks, that, in Ransome's words, 'I even got a letter from Lenin authorising all the commissars to give me whatever information I asked for.' Ransome and Evgenia continued to work for the Secret Intelligence Service until the Bolsheviks asked Evgenia to go to Britain, smuggling in 1 million roubles worth of precious stones to fund European Communist parties with whom she was to liaise, all her actions of course being monitored by the Security Service. In 1924, having divorced his first wife and married Evgenia,

Ransome settled in the Lake District, writing children's books including *Swallows and Amazons*, for which he is best remembered. He died there in 1967, his mysterious past remaining a closely guarded secret. Other equally famous authors also became spies. Somerset Maugham was sent to Russia in 1917 by the Secret Intelligence Service to collect information about the Bolshevik threat. Maugham correctly judged that the government of the moderate Alexander Kerensky would be unable to resist the Bolshevik threat and later used his experience in his series of short stories about the fictional spy *Ashenden* which influenced Ian Fleming, creator of James Bond. Graham Greene spent much of World War II as a bored and not very effective spy in Sierra Leone where he set his novel *The Heart of the Matter* and he drew on his experiences to satirize the profession of spy in his comic novel *Our Man in Havana*.

Local Heroes
Honoured at the pub

Surely one of the greatest honours that can befall a British citizen is to have a pub named after him, or occasionally her. It's not too difficult if you are royal or a war hero (Queen Victoria, Lord Nelson and the Iron Duke being particularly prominent in the field) but it's quite tricky if you start and end life as a commoner. However, a few have made it, mostly local heroes.

The Robert Kett, Wymondham, Norfolk

Robert Kett (1492–1549) was a wealthy inhabitant of the small town of Wymondham, who led a rebellion against the enclosure of Common Land and Open Fields. He was captured, tried for High Treason at the Tower of London and hanged but remains a hero in Norfolk.

OPEN FIELDS REMAIN OPEN

Open fields were a way of ensuring that good and poor land was divided evenly amongst the farmers of a village. One large field was divided into strips which were a furlong (220 yards) long and a chain (22 yards) wide – a distance later chosen for the length of a cricket pitch. One farmer would own several strips scattered throughout the

Open field plan

field. There were usually three fields on which crops would be rotated. It wasn't a very efficient form of agriculture since it encouraged small-scale production, and the enclosure movement, which gathered pace in Tudor times, organized the open fields into much larger units for individual landowners. Further enclosures followed in the Victorian period but the village of Laxton, in Nottinghamshire, retains the system.

Sexey's Arms, Blackford, near Cheddar, Somerset

Hugh Sexey (1556–1619) was born in Bruton, Somerset, taught himself law and in 1599 was appointed as royal auditor to the Exchequer of Elizabeth I. When he died the trustees of his will set up Sexey's Hospital in Bruton to care for the elderly. Part of the site is now occupied by Sexey's School which was founded in 1889 and has the unusual distinction of being a state boarding school. So Hugh Sexey has the most unusual distinction of having a school, a hospital and a pub named after him.

The Alice Lisle, Ringwood, Hampshire

Alice Lisle (c.1614–85) was condemned to death by the notorious Judge Jeffreys for sheltering a supporter of the Duke of Monmouth after his defeat at the battle of Sedgemoor in 1685. Jeffreys sentenced her to be burnt at the stake but she was spared this ordeal and beheaded a few days later at the age of 70. She is one of very few women not of royal blood to have a pub named after her. Another is:

The Martha Gunn, Brighton

Martha Gunn (1726–1815) was a fisherwoman of Brighton who worked as a 'dipper' for the Prince

doctor. Sentenced to hang, he threw a party at Newgate at which he entertained seven prostitutes to a meal in high spirits. Three days later, on 30th November 1774, he was hanged at Tyburn, wearing a new green suit specially made for the occasion.

NO LONGER 'PROPER CHARLIES'

Bow Street Runners were set up by Henry Fielding (1707–1754), playwright, novelist (Tom Jones) and a notably honest magistrate who in 1748 was appointed to sit at Bow Street, Covent Garden. This remained a magistrates' court until 2006 when it was closed. Fielding was determined to eliminate the corruption that had infected the judicial system and the ineffective system of 'constables' set up during the reign of Charles II, which consisted largely of elderly and infirm men and which has given us the expression 'proper Charlies'. Fielding instituted the systematic investigation of crime by appointing honest, fit and salaried 'runners' and by introducing identity parades. His half brother John Fielding (1721–1780) added a mounted force. Between them they

Regent, later George IV. She would forcibly plunge him into the chilly depths of Brighton's seawater. Along with a male dipper called 'Old Smokey', she became a favourite of George IV and may have provided him with 'other services' than those of a dipper.

The Sixteen String Jack, Theydon Bois, Essex

John 'Jack' Rann (1750–74) was a highwayman who laced his knee breeches with sixteen silk laces, thus earning himself the name Sixteen String Jack. In 1774 he was identified by one of the new Bow Street Runners as having stolen a sum of money and a pocket watch from a *may be regarded as the architects of a modern police service. The oldest service of all is the Thames River Police, created by a group of dockland merchants in 1798, followed by the Metropolitan Police which began work on 26th September 1829.*

The Daniel Lambert, Stamford, Lincolnshire

Daniel Lambert (1770–1809), like George IV, was noted for his heroic girth. At the time of his sudden death he was 5 feet 11 inches tall, weighed 52 stone 11 pounds, measured 37 inches round each thigh and 112 inches round his waist. He died in an inn called the Wagon and Horses,

since closed, but is commemorated in a nearby pub which was named in his honour.

The Thomas Lord, West Meon, near Petersfield, Hampshire

Thomas Lord (1755–1832) was a professional cricketer who founded a ground for the aristocratic White Conduit Club in Marylebone. The club changed its name to the Marylebone Cricket Club (MCC) and the rest is history. Thomas Lord retired, a wealthy man, in 1830 to West Meon where he is buried and where the pub is named after its most famous resident who also gave his name to the most famous cricket ground in the world. The ground retained the name of Lord's even after Thomas Lord had sold it for £5,000 to William Ward, a member of the club and a director of the Bank of England. Ward had learned that Lord was planning to sell the ground for housing. It so easily could have been called Ward's instead of Lord's.

OTHER TITLES IN OUR **AMAZING AND EXTRAORDINARY FACTS** SERIES

Amazing and Extraordinary Facts
Series: Kings & Queens
Malcolm Day
ISBN: 978-1 -910821-213

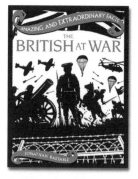

Amazing and Extraordinary Facts Series:
The British At War
Jonathan Bastable
ISBN: 978-1 -910821-237

Amazing and Extraordinary Facts
Series: London
Stephen Halliday
ISBN: 978-1 -910821-022

Amazing and Extraordinary Facts
Series: Scotland
Douglas Skelton
ISBN: 978-1 -910821-145

For more great books visit our website at **www.rydonpublishing.co.uk**

INDEX